EXECUTIVE SUMMARY

Thailand is a constitutional monarchy, with the king serving as head of state. King Bhumibol Adulyadej held this role until his death on October 13. On December 10, his son, King Maha Vajiralongkorn Bodindradebayavarangkun, became head of state. In a 2014 bloodless coup, military and police leaders, taking the name National Council for Peace and Order (NCPO) and led by army chief General Prayut Chan-o-cha, overthrew the civilian government administered by the Puea Thai political party, which had governed since 2011 following National Assembly lower house elections that were generally considered free and fair. After the 2014 coup, citizens no longer had the ability to choose their government through free and fair elections.

The military-led NCPO maintained control over the security forces and all government institutions.

The interim constitution, promulgated by the NCPO in 2014, granted immunity to coup leaders and their subordinates for any pre-coup or post-coup actions ordered by the ruling council, regardless of the legality of the action. The NCPO oversaw a lengthy process for developing a new constitution, which voters approved in an August 7 national referendum. The interim constitution remained in effect at year's end, with the 2016 draft constitution awaiting promulgation with the signature of King Maha Vajiralongkorn. The 2016 constitution stipulates the NCPO remain in office and hold all powers granted by the interim constitution until establishment of a new council of ministers and its assumption of office following the first general election under the new charter. Numerous NCPO decrees limiting civil liberties, including restrictions on freedoms of speech, assembly, and the press, remained in effect during the year. NCPO Order No. 3/2015 grants the military government sweeping power to curb "acts deemed harmful to national peace and stability." The 2016 constitution also stipulates all NCPO orders are "constitutional and lawful" and will remain in effect until revoked by the NCPO, an order from the military-appointed legislative body, the prime minister, or cabinet resolution.

In addition to limitations on civil liberties imposed by the NCPO, the most persistent human rights problems were abuses by government security forces in the continuing ethnic Malay-Muslim insurgency in the southernmost provinces of Yala, Narathiwat, Pattani, and parts of Songkhla, and excessive use of force by government security forces, including harassing or abusing criminal suspects, detainees, and prisoners.

Other human rights problems included arbitrary arrests and detention; poor, overcrowded, and unsanitary prison and detention facilities; insufficient protection for vulnerable populations, including refugees; corruption; violence and discrimination against women; sex tourism; sexual exploitation of children; trafficking in persons; discrimination against persons with disabilities, minorities, hill tribe members, and foreign migrant workers; child labor; and some limitations on worker rights.

Authorities occasionally dismissed, arrested, prosecuted, and convicted security force members who committed abuses. Official impunity, however, continued to be a serious problem, especially in the southernmost provinces, where the Emergency Decree on Public Administration in the State of Emergency (2005), hereinafter referred to as "the emergency decree," and the 2008 Internal Security Act remained in effect.

Insurgents in the southernmost provinces committed human rights abuses and attacks on civilian targets, including in provinces outside their traditional conflict area.

Section 1. Respect for the Integrity of the Person, Including Freedom from:

a. Arbitrary Deprivation of Life or other Unlawful or Politically Motivated Killings

Reports continued, although less than in previous years, that security forces at times used excessive and lethal force against criminal suspects and committed or were involved in extrajudicial, arbitrary, and unlawful killings. According to the Ministry of Interior's Investigation and Legal Affairs Bureau, from October 2015 to September, security forces--including police, military, and other agencies--killed eight suspects during the arrest process, a decrease of nearly 50 percent from the previous year.

There were no reports the government or its agents committed politically motivated killings during the year. There were reports of killings in connection with the conflict in the southernmost provinces (see section 1.g.).

b. Disappearance

There were no reports of politically motivated disappearances. Prominent disappearance cases from prior years remain unsolved. In October the Department of Special Investigations (DSI) announced suspension of its investigation into the presumed enforced disappearance of human rights lawyer Somchai Neelapaijit, who went missing in 2004 while representing several clients who had accused security forces of torture.

As of September the government had not taken action on the 2011 request for a country visit by the UN working group on enforced or involuntary disappearances.

c. Torture and Other Cruel, Inhuman, or Degrading Treatment or Punishment

The interim constitution enacted following the 2014 coup protects "all human dignity, rights, [and] liberties," but does not specifically prohibit torture. The 2016 constitution states, "Torture, acts of brutality, or punishment by cruel or inhumane means shall not be permitted." The emergency decree and the interim constitution effectively provide immunity from prosecution to security officers for actions committed during the performance of their duties. As of September the cabinet had renewed the emergency decree in the southernmost provinces for consecutive three-month periods 45 times since 2005.

Representatives of nongovernmental organizations (NGOs) and legal entities reported police and military officers sometimes tortured and beat suspects to obtain confessions, and newspapers reported numerous cases of citizens accusing police and other security officers of brutality. There were criminal actions pursued against Royal Thai Police (RTP) officers. From October 2015 to August, the RTP disciplinary division reported authorities subjected 3,139 police officers to disciplinary actions, an increase from 2015. Disciplinary offenses included misbehavior, dereliction of duty, harming people or suspects, drunkenness, drug use, embezzlement, gambling, illegal weapons possession, and dishonesty. The investigations resulted in dismissal of 221 officers and other disciplinary action against the remaining 2,918 officers. The RTP reported nine cases of "harming people or suspects" in 2015 but reported no such cases through October. In November police officials filed charges against seven police officers in Huai Kwang District accused of fatally beating the suspected head of a local gambling network.

In January a consortium of human rights groups published a report detailing 54 cases of alleged torture and other cruel, inhuman, or degrading treatment committed by police and military officials in the country's southernmost provinces during 2014-15. The report claimed the incidents occurred mainly at the Ingkayuthaborihan Military Camp in Pattani Province and the Southern Police Operations Center in Yala Province. In May military officials filed a criminal defamation complaint against three of the report's authors (see section 2.a.). In September, Amnesty International released a report documenting 74 alleged cases of torture or mistreatment throughout the country, most occurring after the 2014 coup.

There were numerous reports of hazing and physical abuse by members of military units. In April the Office of the United Nations High Commissioner for Human Rights (OHCHR) reported that one private was killed and another seriously injured at Phayak Military Camp in Yala Province after fellow soldiers severely beat them in apparent retaliation for committing disciplinary offenses.

Prison and Detention Center Conditions

Conditions in prisons and various detention centers--including drug rehabilitation facilities and immigration detention centers (IDCs) where authorities detained undocumented migrants, refugees, and asylum seekers--remained poor, and most were overcrowded. The Ministry of Justice's Department of Corrections is responsible for monitoring prison conditions, while the Ministry of Interior's Immigration Department monitors conditions in IDCs.

The military government held some civilian suspects at military detention facilities.

<u>Physical Conditions</u>: As of September 1, authorities held approximately 306,000 persons in prisons and detention facilities with a maximum design capacity of 210,000 to 220,000 persons.

In some prisons sleeping accommodations were insufficient, and the lack of medical care was a serious problem. Authorities at times transferred seriously ill prisoners and detainees to provincial or state hospitals.

Unsatisfactory prison conditions contributed to prisoners rioting in at least one prison. On July 16, 200 inmates rioted in Pattani Central Prison to protest the prison's strict rules and inmate transfer policy and to demand the transfer of the facility's director. The riot resulted in three deaths and 10 injuries. Asvira Doloh, one of two prisoners accused of instigating the riot, was subsequently transferred to Songkhla Central Prison, where he was found dead in his cell from internal injuries on July 21.

Pretrial detainees comprised approximately 18 percent of the prison population. Prison officers did not segregate these detainees from the general prison population. The government often held pretrial detainees under the emergency decree in the southernmost provinces in military camps or police stations rather than in prisons.

NGOs reported that authorities occasionally held men, women, and children together in police station cells, particularly in small or remote police stations, pending indictment.

In IDCs authorities held male and female detainees together and placed juveniles older than 14 years with adults. Authorities can hold detainees and their children in IDCs for years unless they pay a fine and the cost of their transportation home, because by law "…the alien will have to pay the expense of deportation…[and] [t]he expense of detention shall be charged to the alien's account." NGOs urged the government to enact legislation and policies to end detention of children who are out of visa status and adopt alternatives, such as supervised release and noncustodial, community-based housing, while resolving their immigration status. Other NGOs reported complaints, especially by Muslim detainees in IDCs, of inadequate and culturally inappropriate food. There also were persistent reports of forced labor, extortion by guards, and poor facility ventilation.

Prison authorities sometimes used solitary confinement of not more than one month, as permitted by law, to punish male prisoners who consistently violated prison regulations or were a danger to others. The Department of Corrections reported that solitary confinement averaged approximately seven days. Authorities also used heavy leg irons on prisoners deemed escape risks or potentially dangerous to other prisoners.

According to the Ministry of Interior's Investigation and Legal Affairs Bureau, 762 persons died in official custody from October 2015 to September, including eight deaths while in police custody and 728 in the custody of the Department of Corrections, a 15 percent decrease from the previous year. Authorities attributed most of the deaths to natural causes. Human rights groups reported deficiencies in official investigations into deaths in custody.

The law classifies drug users as patients rather than criminals, and the government may detain persons who use drugs in compulsory rehabilitation centers for either 120 or 180 days to convert drug addicts into "decent citizens." These centers, a joint project of the Ministries of Justice, Interior, and Public Health as well as the armed forces and the RTP, were located in approximately 57 military camps and 29 civilian centers. The centers processed 10,000 to 15,000 persons as of September. Military personnel with no medical background operated most centers.

Department of Probation authorities contended the government periodically evaluated the effectiveness of its drug-cessation operations, and medical personnel or a medical team visited many military camps at least once a week. Prior to detention local authorities made no individual clinical assessments of the severity of drug dependence and afforded no due process. After release authorities typically did not offer patients follow-up treatment. Media reports catalogued abuses of addict detainees, including physical abuse. Health services, such as medically assisted detoxification; HIV prevention, treatment, care, and support; and evidence-based drug dependence treatment, were unavailable.

Administration: Authorities permitted prisoners and detainees or their representatives to submit complaints without censorship to ombudspersons but not directly to judicial authorities. Ombudspersons in turn could consider and investigate complaints and petitions received from prisoners and provide recommendations to the Department of Corrections, but they are not empowered to act on a prisoner's behalf, nor may they involve themselves in a case unless a person files an official complaint. Authorities rarely investigated complaints and did not make public the results of such investigations.

IDCs, administered by the Immigration Police Bureau, which reports to the RTP, are not subject to many of the regulations that govern the regular prison system.

Independent Monitoring: The government facilitated monitoring of prisons by the National Human Rights Commission of Thailand (NHRCT), including meetings with prisoners without third parties present and repeated visits. According to human rights groups, no external or international inspection of the prison system occurred, including of military facilities, such as Bangkok's 11th Military Circle. International organizations reported cooperating with military and police agencies regarding international policing standards and the exercise of police powers.

Representatives of international organizations generally had access to some detainees in IDCs across the country for service delivery and resettlement processing.

d. Arbitrary Arrest or Detention

NCPO Order 2/2558 grants the military authority to detain persons without charge or trial for up to seven days. Military officials frequently invoked this authority. According to OHCHR the military government summoned, arrested, and detained approximately 1,500 persons since the 2014 coup. Prior to releasing detainees, military authorities often required them to sign documents affirming they were treated well, would refrain from political activity, and would seek authorization prior to travel outside the local area. According to human rights groups, authorities often denied access to detainees by family members and attorneys. Military authorities threatened those who failed to respond to summonses with prison and seizure of assets.

The emergency decree, which gives the government authority to detain persons without charge for a maximum of 30 days in unofficial places of detention, remained in effect in the southernmost provinces (see section 1.g.).

Emergency decree provisions make it very difficult to challenge a detention before a court. Under the decree detainees have access to legal counsel, but there was no assurance of prompt access to counsel or family members, nor were there transparent safeguards against the mistreatment of detainees. Moreover, the decree effectively provides broadly based immunity from criminal, civil, and disciplinary liability for officials acting under its provisions.

Role of the Police and Security Apparatus

The law gives military forces authority over civilian institutions, including police, regarding the maintenance of public order. NCPO Order 13/2016, issued in March, grants military officers with the rank of lieutenant and higher power to summon, arrest, and detain suspects; conduct searches; seize assets; suspend financial transactions; and ban suspects from traveling abroad in cases related to 27 criminal offenses, including extortion, human trafficking, robbery, forgery, fraud, defamation, gambling, prostitution, and firearms violation. The order also grants criminal, administrative, civil, and disciplinary immunity to military officials executing police authority in "good faith."

The Border Patrol Police have special authority and responsibility in border areas to combat insurgent movements.

There were reports police abused prisoners and detainees, generally with impunity.

Complaints of police abuse may be filed directly with the superior of the accused police officer, the Office of the Inspector General, or the police commissioner general. The NHRCT, the Lawyers' Council of Thailand (LCT), the Office of the National Anti-Corruption Commission (NACC), the Supreme Court of Justice, the Ministry of Justice, and the Office of the Prime Minister accepted complaints of police abuse and corruption, as did the Office of the Ombudsman. The complaint center of the Department of Rights and Liberties Protection of the Ministry of Justice reported it received 60 complaints of police abuse from October 2015 to September. The Office of the Ombudsman reported receiving 565 petitions alleging police abuse, a 20 percent increase from the previous year.

When police receive a complaint, standard procedures require an internal investigation committee to take up the matter, and it may suspend the officer involved in the complaint for the duration of the investigation. Various administrative penalties exist, and authorities may refer serious cases to a criminal court.

Few complaints resulted in punishment of alleged offenders, and there were numerous examples of investigations lasting years without resolution of alleged security force abuses. Human rights groups criticized the "superficial nature" of police and judicial investigations into incidents of alleged torture and other mistreatment by security forces.

Local police departments are obligated to investigate each case of security force killings and evaluate whether the killings occurred in the line of duty or were otherwise justifiable. The Ministry of Interior's Investigation and Legal Affairs Bureau reported eight killings of civilians during police operations from October 2015 to September. The office also reported 34 deaths of persons in police custody during the same period.

Procedures for investigating suspicious deaths, including deaths occurring in police custody, require a prosecutor, forensic pathologist, and local administrator to participate in the investigation and that, in most cases, family members have legal representation at the inquests. Authorities often failed to follow these procedures.

Families rarely took advantage of a provision of law that allows them to sue police for criminal action during arrests.

In August, Thawatchai Anukun, a former Ministry of Interior official, died while in the custody of the DSI. Officials initially reported Thawatchai hanged himself with his socks while inside a DSI detention cell, but an autopsy revealed he died due to "abdominal hemorrhaging and a ruptured liver from being struck by a blunt object, together with asphyxiation from hanging."

The Ministry of Defense requires service members to receive human rights training. Routine training occurred at various levels, including for officers, noncommissioned officers, enlisted personnel, and recruits. Furthermore, military service members deploying in support of counterinsurgency operations in the southernmost provinces received specific human rights training, including training for detailed, situation-specific contingencies.

Arrest Procedures and Treatment of Detainees

With few exceptions the law requires police and military officers exercising law enforcement authority to obtain a warrant from a judge prior to making an arrest. Issuance of arrest warrants was subject to a judicial tendency to approve automatically all requests for warrants. By law, authorities must inform persons of likely charges against them immediately after arrest and allow them to inform someone of their arrest.

The law provides for access to counsel for criminal detainees in both civilian and military courts, but lawyers and human rights groups claimed police often conducted interrogations without providing access to an attorney. In the southernmost provinces, lawyers reported that, under the emergency decree, authorities denied them adequate access to detained clients, and some persons reported authorities denied them permission to visit detained family members.

Authorities sometimes pressured foreign detainees, especially migrant workers and those in the country illegally, to sign confessions without the benefit of a competent interpreter/translator.

Through July the Ministry of Justice and the Court of Justice assigned volunteer attorneys at public expense in 14,068 legal cases for indigent detainees. Lawyers said fees offered for such service were often low.

The law provides defendants the right to request bail, and the government generally respected this right. Nevertheless, some human rights groups reported police frequently did not inform detained suspects of their right to request bail or refused to recommend bail after suspects submitted a request, particularly in drug arrests and cases involving violence in the southernmost provinces.

Arbitrary Arrest: Under NCPO order 3/2015, the military has authority to detain persons without charge for a maximum of seven days without judicial review. Under the emergency decree, authorities may detain a person for a maximum of 30 days without charge (see section 1.g.). Military officers invoked NCPO Order No. 3/2015 authority to detain numerous government officials, politicians, academics, journalists, and other persons without charge, although reportedly far fewer than in 2015. The military held most individuals briefly but held some for up to seven days.

Pretrial Detention: Under normal conditions the law allows police to detain criminal suspects for 48 hours after arrest for investigation. Lawyers reported police rarely brought cases to court within the 48-hour period. Laws and regulations place offenses for which the maximum penalty for conviction is less than three years under the jurisdiction of district courts, which have different procedures and require police to submit cases to public prosecutors within 72 hours of arrest. According to the LCT, pretrial detention of criminal suspects for as long as 60 days was common.

Before charging and trial, authorities may detain individuals for a maximum of 84 days (for the most serious offenses), with a judicial review required for each seven-day period. After formal charge and throughout trial, depending on prosecution and defense readiness, court caseload, and the nature of the evidence, detention may last for one to two years before a verdict and up to six years before a Supreme Court appellate review. The time a defendant spent in detention prior to sentencing occasionally equaled or exceeded the sentence for the alleged crime.

Detainee's Ability to Challenge Lawfulness of Detention before a Court: Persons arrested or detained by police are entitled to judicial review of their detention within 48 hours in most cases. Persons detained by military officials acting under authority granted by NCPO Order 3/2015 are entitled to judicial review of their detention within seven days. Detainees found by the court to have been detained unlawfully (more than 48 hour or seven days) are entitled to compensation.

<u>Protracted Detention of Rejected Asylum Seekers or Stateless Persons</u>: Authorities detained asylum seekers and refugees without legal status. NGOs alleged the detentions were protracted and that detention conditions failed to meet satisfactory standards.

<u>Amnesty</u>: The Department of Corrections' Pardon Section reported an August 8 Royal Pardon Decree, issued in commemoration of the 70th anniversary of King Bhumibol's ascension to the throne and Queen Sirikit's 84th birthday, granted amnesty to approximately 30,000 convicted persons and reduced the sentences of another 70,000 prisoners. A December 10 royal pardon, issued in conjunction with the ascension of King Maha Vajiralongkorn, granted amnesty to approximately 30,000 additional convicted persons and reduced the sentences of another approximately 70,000 prisoners.

e. Denial of Fair Public Trial

Both the interim constitution and the 2016 constitution provide for an independent judiciary, although the NCPO issued orders that prohibited members of the judiciary from making any negative public comments against the NCPO. Moreover, the interim constitution provides the NCPO power to intervene "regardless of its effects on the legislative, executive, or judiciary" to defend the country against national security threats.

Human rights groups remained concerned about the NCPO's influence on independent judicial processes, particularly the practice of prosecuting some civilians in military courts. According to these groups, the lack of progress in several high-profile cases involving alleged police and military abuse diminished public trust in the justice system and discouraged some victims of human rights abuses (or their families) from seeking justice.

Trial Procedures

The law provides for the presumption of innocence. A single judge decides trials for misdemeanors; regulations require two or more judges for more serious cases. Prior to its suspension, the 2007 constitution provided for a prompt trial, although a large backlog of cases remained in the court system. Most trials are public; however, the court may order a closed trial, particularly in cases involving national security, the royal family, children, or sexual abuse.

In ordinary criminal courts, defendants enjoy a broad range of legal rights, including access to a lawyer of their choosing, prompt and detailed information of the charges against them, free interpretation as necessary from the moment charged through all appeals, the right to be present at trial, and have adequate time and facilities to prepare a defense. They also have the rights not to be compelled to testify or confess guilt, to confront witnesses, and to present witnesses. Authorities did not automatically provide indigent defendants with counsel at public expense, and there were allegations authorities did not afford defendants all the above rights, especially in small or remote provinces.

In a 2014 order, the NCPO redirected prosecutions for offenses against the monarchy, insurrection, sedition, weapons offenses, and violation of its orders from civilian criminal courts to military courts. On September 12, the NCPO ordered an end to the practice, directing that offenses committed by civilians after that date would no longer be subject to military court jurisdiction. At the time of the order, the NCPO explained that approximately 500 pending civilian cases would continue in military courts, as would any other cases in which the alleged crimes were committed before September 12. According to government and NGO sources, from May 2014 to May, military courts initiated at least 1,546 cases against civilians involving at least 1,811 persons, most commonly for violations of Article 112 (lese majeste, defaming or insulting the king, queen, heir-apparent, or regent); failure to comply with an NCPO order; and violations of the law controlling firearms, ammunition, and explosives.

Military courts do not provide the same legal protections for civilian defendants as do civilian criminal courts. Military courts do not afford civilian defendants rights outlined by the interim constitution or the 2016 constitution to a fair and public hearing by a competent, impartial, and independent tribunal. Prior to May 2015, civilians had to seek private counsel from among the limited number of lawyers who were able and willing to take their cases in military court. Civilians facing trial for offenses allegedly committed from May 2014 to April 2015--the period of martial law--have no right of appeal.

In civilian court cases, the government provided legal aid on an intermittent, voluntary basis, but the aid reportedly was of low quality. The LCT budget remained the same as in previous years, approximately 50 million baht ($1.40 million). Some NGOs reported that legal aid lawyers pressured their clients to pay additional fees directly to them, but the LCT's lawyer etiquette division explained clients must pay certain expenses, such as travel, incurred by their attorney. The law requires the court to appoint an attorney in cases where the defendant disputes the charges, is indigent, or is a minor, and in cases where the possible punishment is more than five years' imprisonment or death. Most free legal aid came from private groups, including the LCT and the Thai Women Lawyers' Association.

There is no pretrial discovery process; consequently, lawyers and defendants do not have access to evidence prior to trial. The law provides for access to courts or administrative bodies to appeal or seek redress, and the government generally respected this right.

Several NGOs expressed concern about the lack of adequate protection for witnesses, particularly in cases involving alleged police wrongdoing. The Office of Witness Protection of the Ministry of Justice had limited resources and primarily played a coordinating role. In most cases police provided witness protection, but six other state agencies also participated in the program: the Ministry of Defense; the Office of the Narcotic Control Board; and the departments of special investigations, provincial administration, juvenile observation and protection, and corrections.

Police forced pretrial criminal suspects to re-enact their alleged crimes in the presence of media, victims and their families, and the public. Media widely published and broadcast images from these re-enactments on an almost daily basis. Police often ordered suspects to perform certain actions consistent with the crime's circumstances. Police conducted thousands of re-enactments during the year. Although police regulations require suspects to "confess" before re-enactments, police often obtained these "confessions" by coercion, including physical assault. Persons present at re-enactments physically assaulted or attempted to physically assault suspects on at least six separate occasions during the first eight months of the year. Human rights organizations criticized forced re-enactments because they violated the presumption of innocence and encouraged violence against suspects.

Political Prisoners and Detainees

The NCPO routinely detained those who expressed political views (see section 1.d.). As of March the Department of Corrections reported there were 103 persons detained or imprisoned in the country under lese majeste laws that outlaw criticism of the monarchy (see section 2.a.). Human rights groups claimed the prosecutions and convictions of several lese majeste offenders were politically motivated. Police arrested student activist Jatupat Boonpattararaksa in December for "liking" and sharing on Facebook a link to a Thai-language BBC profile of the new king that allegedly contained defamatory information. On December 22, a court revoked Jatupat's bail and rearrested him on charges he continued to use social media to taunt officials.

Civil Judicial Procedures and Remedies

The law provides for access to courts and administrative bodies to sue for damages for, or cessation of, a human rights violation. The government generally respected this right, but the emergency decree in force in the southernmost provinces expressly excludes administrative court scrutiny or civil or criminal proceedings against government officials. Victims may seek compensation from a government agency instead.

f. Arbitrary or Unlawful Interference with Privacy, Family, Home, or Correspondence

Prior to the 2014 coup, the constitution prohibited such actions with some exceptions, and the government generally respected these prohibitions. Following the coup the NCPO repealed the constitution and implemented martial law, which it later rescinded and replaced with NCPO Order No. 3/2015, issued under Article 44 of the NCPO-imposed interim constitution. These provisions, along with the emergency decree, give government security forces authority to conduct warrantless searches that they used routinely in the southernmost provinces and other border areas. There were complaints during the year from persons who claimed security forces abused this authority.

There were reports military officers harassed family members of those suspected of opposing the NCPO, including parents of students involved in anti-NCPO protests and the families of human rights defenders. For example, in July the RTP raided the home of the Thai wife of a foreign journalist who published an article critical of the monarchy. Officials arrested the wife and subjected her to six hours of interrogation before releasing her. In another case, human rights groups claimed military officials arrested and charged the mother of a prominent anti-coup activist with violating lese majeste provisions to try to pressure her son to stop his political activity.

Security services monitored persons, including foreign visitors, who espoused highly controversial views.

g. Abuses in Internal Conflicts

Internal conflict continued in the ethnic Malay-Muslim-majority, southernmost provinces. Because of frequent attacks by suspected insurgents as well as government security operations, tension between the local ethnic Malay-Muslim and ethnic Thai-Buddhist communities remained high, alongside the local population's persistent distrust of security officers.

The emergency decree in effect in the southern border provinces of Yala, Pattani, Narathiwat, and parts of Songkhla, provides military, police, and civilian authorities significant powers to restrict some basic rights and delegates certain internal security powers to the armed forces. The decree also provides security forces broad immunity from prosecution. Moreover, martial law--imposed in 2006--remained in effect and significantly empowered security forces in the southernmost provinces (see section 1.d.).

Killings: According to NGO Deep South Watch, there were 16 reported cases of government-affiliated forces conducting extrajudicial killings in the southernmost provinces as of December.

According to Deep South Watch, violence resulted in 212 deaths and 441 injuries in 593 incidents as of August, more than in 2015. It also reported that, as of August, violence caused 6,486 deaths and injured 11,793 persons in 15,968 incidents in the region since 2004, but the organization did not differentiate among violence caused by insurgents, security forces, or criminal elements. As in previous years, suspected insurgents frequently targeted government representatives, including district and municipal officials, military personnel, and police, with bombings and shootings. Deep South Watch noted a recent trend of violence, most likely perpetrated by insurgents, against soft targets such as businesses, medical institutions, and schools. According to media reports, suspected insurgents killed one teacher and one student, a decrease from 2015. Insurgents also killed and injured both Buddhist and Muslim civilians from many other occupations.

Some government-backed civilian defense volunteers received basic training and weapons from security forces. Human rights organizations continued to express concerns about vigilantism by these defense volunteers and other civilians.

Abductions: The Muslim Attorney Center received one report of an enforced disappearance by government security forces in the southern border provinces. Other human rights organizations noted difficulties in collecting information amid widespread government summonses and detentions.

<u>Physical Abuse, Punishment, and Torture</u>: The government arrested suspected insurgents, some of them juveniles, and in some cases held them for a month or more under emergency decree and martial law provisions. As of September 20, the Muslim Attorney Center received 18 complaints from insurgent suspects alleging torture by the military. The Cross Cultural Foundation reported the death of one prisoner in the southernmost provinces that occurred during a prison transfer. Human rights organizations maintained the detention of suspects continued to be arbitrary, excessive, and needlessly lengthy and criticized overcrowded conditions at detention facilities.

Martial law allows detention for a maximum of seven days without charge and without court or government agency approval in the southernmost provinces. The emergency decree in effect in the same areas allows authorities to arrest and detain suspects for a maximum of 30 days without charge. After this period expires, authorities may begin holding suspects under normal criminal law (see section 1.d.). Unlike under martial law, detentions under normal criminal law require court consent, although human rights NGOs complained courts did not always exercise their right of review. In some cases authorities held suspects first under martial law for seven days and then detained them for an additional 30 days under the decree. The Southern Border Provinces Operation Center reported through September authorities arrested 79 persons via warrants issued under the emergency decree. The government did not use military courts to try civilian defendants in the southernmost provinces.

<u>Child Soldiers</u>: Regulations prohibit formal recruitment of children younger than 18 years to serve as Territorial Defense Volunteers, and volunteers generally joined at age 21 years or older. The Cross Cultural Foundation noted some children younger than 18 years were observed working with their fathers or relatives at village defense checkpoints. As recently as 2015, there were reports insurgent groups recruited children younger than 18 years to commit acts of arson or serve as scouts.

Also see the Department of State's *Trafficking in Persons Report* at www.state.gov/j/tip/rls/tiprpt/.

<u>Other Conflict-related Abuses</u>: After several years of declining violence against civilians, human rights groups noted an increase in insurgent activity affecting civilians. On March 13, a group of approximately 50 armed men, who authorities believed were insurgents, seized a hospital building in Narathiwat and exchanged

gunfire with a government paramilitary base located adjacent to the hospital. Seven government rangers were wounded in the attack, although no casualties were reported among patients and hospital personnel, and the facility suffered extensive damage. On August 11-12, a series of coordinated bombings and arson attacks targeting tourist sites outside of the southernmost provinces killed four and injured at least 20. On August 23, a bomb placed inside a stolen ambulance detonated outside a hotel in Pattani, killing one and injuring 29 predominantly civilian victims.

The Ministry of Public Health reported attacks on only one public health facility as of August, but there were no deaths or injuries. According to the Ministry of Education, as of August there were no deaths of students, teachers, or other education personnel, although media reported insurgents killed one teacher and one student as of September. The government frequently armed both ethnic Thai-Buddhist and ethnic Malay-Muslim civilian defense volunteers, fortified schools and temples, and provided military escorts to monks and teachers.

Section 2. Respect for Civil Liberties, Including:

a. Freedom of Speech and Press

Broad NCPO orders restricting freedom of speech and press, issued following the 2014 coup, remained in effect at year's end. Invoking these orders, officials suspended media outlets, blocked access to internet sites, and summoned members of media to report to authorities for questioning and "attitude adjustment." In addition to official restrictions on speech and censorship, NCPO actions resulted in significant self-censorship by the public and media. The NCPO prohibited political figures, analysts, and others from providing interviews or comments to media and banned dissemination of information that could threaten the NCPO or "create conflict" within the country, particularly in advance of the August 7 constitutional referendum.

Freedom of Speech and Expression: The NCPO enforced limits on free speech and expression using a variety of regulations and criminal provisions. The Referendum Law, enacted in advance of the August 7 constitutional referendum, criminalized campaigning related to the referendum, and the NCPO used the law almost exclusively to suppress political expression opposed to the draft charter (see section 3). Procharter speech, including comments by senior NCPO officials, was allowed.

The NCPO also invoked criminal sedition statutes to restrict political speech. In April the military charged eight political activists with sedition for posting information on a satirical Facebook page called, "We Love General Prayut."

Article 112 of the criminal code, the so-called lese majeste law, makes it a crime--punishable by a maximum of 15 years' imprisonment for each offense--to criticize, insult, or threaten the king, queen, royal heir apparent, or regent. The government increasingly used this law to prosecute anyone critical of the monarchy or members of the royal family in any way, especially following the October 13 death of King Bhumibol and the December 10 ascension of King Maha Vajiralongkorn. The law also allows citizens to file lese majeste complaints against each other, which they did on numerous occasions. The government regularly conducted lese majeste trials in secret and prohibited public disclosure of the content of the alleged offenses. The government also frequently tried lese majeste cases in military courts that provided fewer rights and protections for civilian defendants, although a September 12 order ended the practice of trying violations of Article 112 in military courts for offenses committed after that date (see section 1.e.). International and domestic human rights organizations and academics expressed concern about the lese majeste law's chilling effect on freedom of expression.

Official statistics varied by agency, but new lese majeste cases increased dramatically following the 2014 coup. According to local NGO Internet Dialogue on Law Reform, the number of new lese majeste cases filed since the 2014 coup was 68 as of September, although police officials acknowledged dozens of additional investigations following King Bhumibol's death on October 13. In some of these cases, the accused committed the alleged offense prior to the 2014 coup, but authorities only filed charges afterwards. According to the Department of Corrections, the government detained 103 persons under lese majeste laws as of March 31 (including a number of persons convicted for corruption-related offenses under Article 112 for misuse of royal title to further business interests).

On March 4, a military prosecutor filed lese majeste charges against Thanakorn Siripaiboon for "liking" a Facebook post deemed critical of the king and for writing a Facebook post referring to the king's dog in a sarcastic manner.

The government also invoked the lese majeste law to censor or ban media publications. On April 8, officials banned the French edition of *Marie Claire* magazine from distribution in the country after it published a story about the royal family, according to an official government announcement.

<u>Press and Media Freedoms</u>: The 2016 constitution requires owners of newspapers and other mass media to be citizens. Government entities owned and controlled most radio and broadcast television stations, including the 524 officially registered AM and FM stations. The armed forces and police owned another 244 radio stations, ostensibly for national security purposes. Other owners of national broadcast media included the government's Public Relations Department and the Mass Communication Organization of Thailand Public Company Limited, a former state enterprise in which the government maintained a majority share. Government entities leased nearly all stations to commercial companies that provided commercial content to the stations.

The law provides for the regulation of radio and television frequencies and three categories of broadcast licenses (public service, community service, and commercial). The National Broadcasting and Telecommunications Commission (NBTC) allocates broadcast frequencies and regulates broadcast media. Radio stations must renew their licenses every seven years. The law requires stations to broadcast 30-minute, government-produced newscasts twice daily and to register with the NBTC. Several thousand small community radio stations countrywide also operated under a separate licensing system that requires annual renewal of licenses.

<u>Violence and Harassment</u>: Senior government officials routinely made statements critical of media. Media operators also complained of harassment and monitoring.

On March 14, plainclothes military personnel monitored and recorded a film screening held at the Foreign Correspondents' Club of Thailand (FCCT), a practice the club's president, Jonathan Head, complained to the government occurred regularly. In response to FCCT complaints, an NCPO spokesperson stated that the monitoring was legal and conducted to verify the club's activities were not part of any political movement.

On July 26, Premsak Piyayura, a mayor and former member of parliament, allegedly had his subordinates in the presence of other journalists pull down the pants of a newspaper reporter who had questioned him about a controversial Facebook posting. The incident drew widespread criticism from media as an example of the lack of respect and mistreatment of journalists by government officials. Using his authority under Article 44 of the interim constitution, Prime Minister Prayut later suspended the mayor without pay pending a formal investigation.

<u>Censorship or Content Restrictions</u>: The NCPO restricted content deemed critical of or threatening to it, and the media widely practiced self-censorship. NCPO orders remained in effect that prohibited any criticism of military authorities and directed print media, television, radio, cable, and other online media operators not to publish or broadcast any information critical of the military's actions or criticism likely to cause public misunderstanding made with malice and false information aimed to discredit the NCPO. Authorities monitored media content from all media sources, including international press.

Many media contacts reported concerns about NCPO orders authorizing government officials to limit press freedom and suspend press operations without a court order. On May 3, World Press Freedom Day, the Thai Journalists' Association and the Thai Broadcast Journalists' Association issued a joint statement asking the NCPO to revoke any laws that limit or violate freedom of the press, including NCPO orders 97/2557, 103/2557, and 3/2558.

While international media operated relatively freely, in February the Ministry of Foreign Affairs issued revised guidelines for issuing visas to journalists and media correspondents. Foreign journalists feared the new guidelines provide discretionary power to deny media visas based on the content of media reporting. According to the FCCT, authorities denied visas to at least five journalists since the 2014 coup.

On September 13, several media organizations petitioned the National Reform Steering Assembly to review a government proposal to form a regulatory organization called the National Media Professional Council to regulate the conduct of media practitioners.

The emergency decree, which remained in effect in the conflict-affected southernmost provinces, empowers the government "to prohibit publication and distribution of news and information that may cause the people to panic or with an intention to distort information." It also authorizes the government to censor news considered a threat to national security.

<u>Libel/Slander Laws</u>: Defamation is a criminal offense punishable by a maximum fine of 200,000 baht ($5,600) and two years' imprisonment. Military and business figures filed criminal defamation and libel cases against political and environmental activists, journalists, and politicians.

There were several high-profile cases of criminal defamation against human rights defenders. In May officials from the military's Internal Security Operations Command Region 4 filed criminal defamation and computer crimes charges against three of the principal drafters of a report documenting cases of alleged torture by security forces in the southernmost provinces. Numerous national and international human rights groups condemned the charges against Pornpen Khongkachonkiet, Anchana Heemmina, and Somchai Homlaor, arguing the charges posed a serious threat to all human rights monitoring and reporting in the country.

In July police in Narathiwat Province charged Naritsarawan Kaewnopparat, the niece of a military conscript killed by fellow soldiers in 2011, with criminal defamation and computer crimes for statements she made demanding the prosecution of soldiers responsible for her uncle's death. An internal army investigation previously found that a junior officer and other conscripts tortured Naritsarawan's uncle and caused his death, although no one was criminally charged.

In another case, the Criminal Court on September 20, found British citizen Andy Hall guilty of criminal defamation and computer crimes, based on a Finnwatch report to which he contributed in 2013 that accused a local food company, Natural Fruit, of human and labor rights violations at its factory in Prachuap Khiri Khan Province. The report claimed the firm paid wages below the legal minimum and subjected workers to dangerous working conditions and excessive hours. Natural Fruit subsequently filed a criminal defamation complaint against Hall in 2014. The court sentenced Hall to three years in prison and a fine, although it suspended the prison sentence.

National Security: Section 44 of the interim constitution, later extended by the 2016 constitution, provides authorities the right to restrict distribution of material deemed to threaten national security. Media associations expressed alarm regarding the sweeping powers they complained lacked clear criteria for determining what constitutes a threat to national security.

On August 29, the NBTC suspended the broadcast of Voice TV's *Wake Up News* program for one week for broadcasting political commentary deemed to violate NCPO orders. Following the suspension announcement, Voice TV executives stated the channel would voluntarily "reduce and tone down its political commentary" to avoid further punishment.

Internet Freedom

The government continued to restrict or disrupt access to the internet, and censored online content. There were reports the government monitored private online communications without appropriate legal authority.

The law establishes procedures for the search and seizure of computers and computer data in certain criminal investigations and gives the information ministry authority to request and enforce the removal of information disseminated via computer. The government may impose a maximum five-year prison sentence and a 100,000 baht ($2,800) fine for posting false content on the internet found to undermine public security, cause public panic, or harm others, based on vague definitions. Authorities may impose a maximum 20-year sentence and 300,000 baht ($8,400) fine if an offense results in the death of a person. The law also obliges internet service providers to preserve all user records for 90 days in case authorities wish to access them. Any service provider that gives consent to or intentionally supports the publishing of illegal content is also liable to punishment. Most prosecutions were for content-related offenses. By law authorities must obtain a court order to ban a website, although officials did not always respect this requirement. Media activists criticized the law, stating it defined offenses too broadly and some penalties were too harsh.

Individuals and groups generally engaged in the peaceful expression of views via the internet, although there were numerous restrictions on content, including proscribing lese majeste, pornography, gambling, and criticism of the NCPO.

The government closely monitored and blocked thousands of websites critical of the monarchy. The successful prosecution of journalists, political activists, and other internet users for criminal defamation for posting content online further fostered an environment of self-censorship. Many political online message boards and discussion forums closely monitored discussions to avoid being blocked. Newspapers disabled or restricted access to their public comment sections to minimize exposure to possible lese majeste or defamation charges. Authorities also lobbied foreign internet content and service providers to remove or locally censor lese majeste content. Human rights contacts reported that police sometimes asked detained political activists to reveal passwords to their social media accounts.

Following the October 13 death of King Bhumibol, the NBTC and other government entities routinely blocked online and broadcast content related to the monarchy. The NBTC also issued instructions encouraging citizens to identify and report any online content that appeared to violate the lese majeste law.

The RTP Technical Crime Suppression Division reported receiving 3,638 complaints from January to September, compared with 2,083 computer-related complaints it reported from January to August 2014 that resulted in 65 criminal actions. Most cases involved alleged defamation, lese majeste, and other illegal activity, such as gambling and pornography.

Internet access was widely available in urban areas and used by citizens, including through a government program to provide limited free Wi-Fi access at 300,000 hotspots in cities and schools. The government also undertook an initiative to expand internet access to rural areas throughout the country. International monitoring groups estimated 29 million citizens (43 percent of the population) had access to the internet during the year.

In December the NCPO-appointed National Legislative Assembly (NLA) unanimously passed an amendment to the 2007 Computer Crimes Act that significantly expanded government powers to control and capture online content and increased criminal sanctions against individuals and internet service providers for false or distorted information posted online.

Academic Freedom and Cultural Events

The NCPO intervened to disrupt academic discussions on college campuses, intimidated scholars, and arrested student leaders critical of the coup. Universities also practiced self-censorship.

In the run-up to the August 7 national referendum on the draft constitution, at least three universities--Khon Kaen University, Mahidol University, and Ubon Ratchatani University--banned public on-campus discussion of the charter. Notwithstanding university policy, students at Khon Kaen University organized a public on-campus discussion of the draft charter. University officials reportedly cut off water and power and removed all chairs in the building where the event was to be held in an effort to stop it. Following the event university staff filed a police complaint accusing the student participants of trespassing.

Election Commission officials reportedly sent a letter to Mahidol University officials complaining that a prominent university faculty member made critical comments about the draft charter. At Ubon Ratchatani University, the dean of the

Political Science Faculty canceled a public seminar on the draft constitution under pressure from both university and provincial officials.

In April military officials forced cancelation of a scheduled discussion program on the draft constitution organized by Book Republic, an independent bookstore in Chiang Mai that regularly organizes discussions on various contemporary issues. On October 5, immigration officials detained and deported Hong Kong democracy activist Joshua Wong, who had traveled to Bangkok to participate in an academic panel at Chulalongkorn University commemorating the October 6, 1976 massacre of student activists at Thammasat University.

University authorities reported the regular presence of military personnel on campus, monitoring lectures and attending student events. There were numerous accounts of authorities arresting students for exercising freedom of speech and expression, particularly in advance of the August 7 referendum.

The military government continued the process of revising secondary and primary school textbooks and increased instruction on patriotic themes. The military government also continued a civic education curriculum emphasizing General Prayut's 12 core values of "Thainess."

Government authorities continued to be sensitive to the content of film and performing arts. Acknowledging government sensitivities, the Thailand International Film Festival 2016 pulled from its lineup four films it feared might present a negative image of the country.

b. Freedom of Peaceful Assembly and Association

Freedom of Assembly

The 2016 constitution grants the freedom to assemble peacefully, subject to restrictions enacted to "protect public interest, peace and order, or good morals, or to protect the rights and liberties of others."

Invoking authority under Article 44 of the interim constitution, coup leaders prohibited political gatherings of five or more persons and penalized persons supporting any political gatherings. Human rights groups argued the prohibition violated the country's obligations under the International Covenant on Civil and Political Rights. The 2015 Public Assembly Act codified restrictions on freedom of assembly and requires, among other provisions, that protesters obtain permission from police for rallies at least 24 hours in advance. Moreover, it bans all demonstrations within 500 feet of the prime minister's headquarters, parliament, royal palaces, and courthouses. The emergency decree in effect in the southernmost provinces also provides authority to limit freedom of assembly.

Police arrested citizens assembled in violation of government orders. According to a government watchdog organization, in advance of the August 7 referendum officials arrested and charged more than 150 persons nationwide for violating the prohibition on political gatherings of five or more persons. While the NCPO enforced bans against political gatherings critical of the coup or the NCPO, authorities allowed some pro-coup and pro-military demonstrations. In August police arrested 19 men for violating a ban on political gatherings after they set up a monitoring center to oversee the August 7 constitutional referendum. On December 16, the attorney general charged all 19 with violating the government's ban and the court accepted the charges. On September 21, local administrators in Pattani Province intervened and stopped approximately 500 people from gathering to celebrate International Peace Day.

Surat Thani, Phuket, and Phang Nga Provinces have their own regulations that prohibit migrant workers--specifically persons from Cambodia, Burma, and Laos-- from gathering in groups, while Samut Sakhon Province prohibits migrant gatherings of more than five persons. Authorities did not enforce these provisions strictly, particularly for gatherings on private property. Employers and NGOs may request permission from authorities for migrant workers to hold cultural gatherings.

Freedom of Association

The interim constitution did not explicitly provide for freedom of association. The 2016 constitution grants individuals the right to free association subject to restrictions by law enacted to "protect public interest, peace and order, or good morals."

The law prohibits the registration of a political party with the same name or logo as a legally dissolved party.

c. Freedom of Religion

See the Department of State's *International Religious Freedom Report* at www.state.gov/religiousfreedomreport/.

d. Freedom of Movement, Internally Displaced Persons, Protection of Refugees, and Stateless Persons

The interim constitution and the 2016 constitution provide for freedom of internal movement, foreign travel, emigration, and repatriation. The government generally respected these rights, with some exceptions for "maintaining the security of the state, public peace and order or public welfare, town and country planning, or youth welfare."

Following the 2014 coup, the NCPO issued orders prohibiting travel outside the country for approximately 155 persons. In May the NCPO lifted the travel ban for approximately 130 of these persons, essentially those who were not otherwise facing criminal charges and subject to judicial travel restrictions. Prior to lifting the travel ban, the NCPO in March refused a request from journalist Pravit Rojanaphruk to travel to Finland to participate in a World Press Freedom Day event.

In addition to those initially subject to travel restrictions by NCPO order, the Thai Lawyers for Human Rights Center (TLHR) estimated there were an additional 300 persons who, when summoned to appear before the NCPO following the 2014 coup, signed agreements as a condition of their release consenting not to travel abroad without NCPO approval. According to the TLHR, the NCPO has not revoked the restrictions contained in these agreements.

The government usually cooperated with the Office of the United Nations High Commissioner for Refugees (UNHCR), the International Organization for Migration, the International Committee of the Red Cross, and other humanitarian organizations in providing protection and assistance to internally displaced persons, refugees, asylum seekers, stateless persons, and other persons of concern, although with some restrictions. Cooperation with UNHCR to protect certain groups remained uneven, which limited UNHCR's ability to provide protection to all nationalities.

Abuse of Migrants, Refugees, and Stateless Persons: Media reports, Human Rights Watch, and other sources alleged government officials took bribes from and colluded with human smugglers and traffickers who detained Rohingya on islands and other locations in the south. In 2015 authorities confined in IDCs and shelters approximately 870 Rohingya and Bangladeshi persons who arrived in the country irregularly by boat during the mass movement in the Bay of Bengal and Andaman

Sea crisis of May 2015. As of December approximately 330 of them (mostly Rohingya) remained in detention.

Authorities continued to treat refugees and asylum seekers from Burma who lived outside of designated border camps, including Rohingya boat arrivals, as illegal migrants. Multidisciplinary teams conducted interviews and identified some of the Rohingya arrivals as victims of trafficking, and officials subsequently transferred them to shelters under the care of the Ministry of Social Development and Human Security. Persons categorized as illegal migrants are legally subject to arrest and detention. The government worked in cooperation with donors and international organization partners to provide protection and assistance to Rohingya while in IDCs and shelters. The lack of Rohingya-speaking interpreters within IDCs and shelters remained a concern. Although reinstated in 2013, authorities implemented inconsistently the practice of permitting bail for detained refugees and asylum seekers originally initiated in 2011.

International humanitarian organizations noted concerns about congested conditions, lack of exercise opportunities, and limited freedom of movement in the IDCs. Some IDCs with Rohingya detainees lacked efficient medical referral mechanisms and failed to allow exercise due to fear the detainees would escape.

Authorities allowed some women and children, including unaccompanied minors whom officials certified were victims of trafficking, to stay in shelters operated by the Ministry of Social Development and Human Security. Persons in these shelters often reported a lack of adequate human resources to meet the needs of running the facilities and providing adequate psychosocial services to shelter residents.

In-country Movement: The government restricted the free internal movement of members of hill tribes and other minority groups who were not citizens but held government-issued identity cards. Authorities prohibited holders of such cards from traveling outside their home districts without prior permission from the district office or outside their home provinces without permission from the provincial governor. Offenders are subject to fines or a jail term of 45 to 60 days. Persons without cards may not travel at all. Human rights organizations reported police at inland checkpoints often asked for bribes in exchange for allowing stateless persons to move from one district to another.

Foreign Travel: Local authorities also required other long-time noncitizen residents, including thousands of ethnic Shan and other non-hill-tribe minorities, to seek permission for foreign travel. A small number of Burmese refugees, who were approved for third-country resettlement but not recognized as refugees by the government because they reside outside the nine refugee camps, have awaited exit permits for years.

Protection of Refugees

The government's treatment of refugees and asylum seekers remained inconsistent. Nevertheless, authorities hosted significant numbers of refugees and asylum seekers, generally provided protection against their expulsion or return, and allowed persons fleeing fighting or other incidents of violence in neighboring countries to cross the border and remain until conflict ceased. Moreover, authorities permitted non-Burmese refugees recognized by UNHCR and registered Burmese refugees residing in official refugee camps to resettle to third countries.

Access to Asylum: The law does not provide for the granting of asylum or refugee status. Burmese asylum seekers and refugees who reside outside official refugee camps are by law considered illegal migrants, as are all non-Burmese asylum seekers and refugees in the country if they do not hold a valid passport and visa. If arrested they are subject to indefinite detention at IDCs in Bangkok and other provinces.

UNHCR remained limited in its ability to provide protection to Lao Hmong, Uighurs, and Burmese outside the official camps as well as to all North Koreans. Its access to asylum seekers in the main IDC in Bangkok and at Suvarnabhumi International Airport to conduct status interviews and monitor new arrivals varied throughout the year. UNHCR had access to provincial IDCs where authorities detained ethnic Rohingya, including coastal Ranong Province and southern Songkhla Province, to conduct refugee status determinations. Authorities allowed resettlement countries to conduct processing activities in the IDCs, and humanitarian organizations were able to provide health care, nutritional support, and other humanitarian assistance.

The government allowed UNHCR to monitor the protection status of approximately 103,000 Burmese refugees and asylum seekers living in nine camps along the border with Burma but prohibited UNHCR from any assistance role in the camps. NGOs funded by the international community provided basic humanitarian assistance in the camps, including health care, food, education, shelter, water, sanitation, vocational training, and other services. UNHCR issued identification cards to registered refugees living in the camps.

The government facilitated resettlement for 3,479 Burmese refugees from camps as of December. Refugees residing in the nine camps along the border who had not registered with the government were ineligible for third-country resettlement.

An estimated 60,000 Burmese had not registered since the cessation of the Provincial Admissions Boards in 2005. In 2012 the government resumed limited admissions screening to consider only refugee cases under the family reunification criteria (parent/child or spousal relationships) through Fast Track Provincial Admission Boards (FTPAB). As of December authorities had received 3,246 cases with 8,208 persons (including 4,467 FTPAB-registered persons).

Refoulement: The government provided some protection against the expulsion or return of refugees to countries where they would face threats to their lives or freedom because of their race, religion, nationality, membership in a particular social group, or political opinion. Outside the camps government officials did not distinguish between asylum-seeking Burmese and other undocumented Burmese, regarding all as illegal migrants. Authorities generally took those arrested outside of the camps to the border and deported them back to their home country. Authorities generally did not deport persons of concern holding valid UNHCR asylum-seeker or refugee status; however, in 2015 authorities forcibly repatriated two Chinese activists to whom UNHCR had granted refugee status, and forcibly deported a vulnerable migrant group of 109 ethnic Uighurs to China. As of December approximately 60 Uighurs remained in detention in the country.

Immigration police in Bangkok arrested and detained asylum seekers and refugees, including women and children. The detained population fluctuated between 250 and 450 persons, depending on immigration raids and the release of detainees on bail. Government officials estimated the IDC in Bangkok repatriated 200 to 300 undocumented immigrant detainees per week. Authorities typically detained Burmese, Cambodian, and Laotian persons for approximately five days before repatriating them. In contrast, authorities often held detainees for a year or longer if they lacked assistance from their respective embassies, sought third-country resettlement, refused to return to their countries of origin, or lacked funds to pay for their trip home.

Freedom of movement: Refugees residing in the nine refugee camps on the border with Burma had no freedom of movement, and authorities confined them to the camps. In previous years authorities did not enforce this policy, and many refugees often left the camps for short periods to find work in the local economy. Following the 2014 coup, camp commanders began enforcing restrictions on camp residents, making freedom of movement outside the camps more difficult. A refugee apprehended outside the official camps is subject to harassment, fines, detention, deregistration, and deportation.

Refugees and asylum seekers were not eligible to participate in the official nationality verification process, which allows migrant workers with verified nationality and passports to travel throughout the country. Authorities restricted those holding only work permits from traveling outside the province where they work unless they first obtained official permission.

Employment: The law prohibits refugees from working in the country. The government allowed undocumented migrant workers from neighboring Burma, Cambodia, and Laos to work legally in certain economic sectors if they registered with authorities and followed a prescribed process to document their status (see section 7.d.). In March the government announced that victims of trafficking who cooperated with pending court cases would receive renewable one-year stay and work permits; however, as of December the program had not been implemented.

Access to Basic Services: The international community provided basic services for refugees living inside the nine camps on the border with Burma. For needs beyond primary care, a complicated medical referral system hampered the ability of refugees to seek some necessary medical services, although coordination among service providers improved the situation. For the urban refugee and asylum seeker population living in Bangkok, access to basic health services was minimal. Since 2014 two NGOs have provided primary and mental health-care services. UNHCR coordinated referrals of the most urgent medical cases to local hospitals.

Since Burmese refugee children living in the camps generally did not have access to the government education system, NGOs provided schooling opportunities, and some were able to coordinate their curriculum with the Ministry of Education. In Bangkok some refugee communities formed their own schools to provide education for their children. Others sought to learn Thai with support from UNHCR, because the law provides that government schools must admit children of any legal status who can speak, read, and write Thai with some degree of proficiency.

Temporary Protection: The government continued to extend temporary protection status to the migrants of Rohingya and Bangladeshi origin who arrived during the 2015 maritime migration crisis in the Bay of Bengal and Andaman Sea.

Stateless Persons

The government continued to identify stateless persons, provide documentation to preclude statelessness, and open paths to citizenship for long-time residents. According to the government, an estimated 487,000 persons, mainly residing in the northern region, were likely stateless or at risk of statelessness. Several NGOs reported that most stateless persons, many of whom were members of hill tribes, might be eligible for citizenship (see section 6). Others were migrants from Burma who did not have evidence of Burmese citizenship, ethnic minorities registered with civil authorities, previously undocumented minorities, and displaced persons residing in border camps. The government announced plans to reduce drastically the number of stateless persons, focusing initially on the citizenship applications of approximately 60,000 children.

Birth within the country does not automatically confer citizenship. The law bases citizenship on birth to at least one citizen parent, marriage to a male citizen, or naturalization. Individuals may also acquire citizenship by means of special government-designated criteria implemented by the Ministry of Interior with approval from the cabinet or in accordance with nationality law (see section 6). Amendments to the law during the year allowed ethnic Thai stateless persons and their children, who meet the added definition of "displaced Thai," to apply for the status of "Thai nationality by birth," but there were reports of slow, inconsistent implementation due to complicated laws and regulations and the existence of substantial gray areas.

The law stipulates every child born in the country receive an official birth certificate regardless of the parents' legal status. Many parents did not obtain birth certificates for their children due to the complexity of the process, the need to travel from remote areas to district offices, and a lack of recognition of the importance of the document.

By law stateless members of hill tribes may not vote or own land, and their travel is restricted. Stateless persons also may not participate in certain occupations reserved for citizens, including farming, although authorities permitted noncitizen members of hill tribes to undertake subsistence agriculture. Stateless persons had difficulty accessing credit and government services, such as health care. Although education was technically accessible for all undocumented and stateless children, it was usually of poor quality. School administrators placed the term "non-Thai citizen" on these students' high school certificates, which severely limited their economic opportunities. Some public universities still charged stateless and undocumented students higher tuition rates than citizens, and administrators commonly denied these students university student loans.

Without legal status stateless persons were particularly vulnerable to various forms of abuse (see section 6).

Section 3. Freedom to Participate in the Political Process

The interim constitution set the framework for the adoption of a new constitution but did not provide citizens the ability to choose their government peacefully. Instead, it established a process in which unelected persons would serve as interim legislators, and the junta appointed a separate body to draft a new constitution. The Constitution Drafting Committee (CDC) drafted a new constitution that establishes procedures under which citizens would once again be able to choose their government. The CDC also set in place procedures for the new constitution's public approval.

In March the CDC released to the public its draft constitution. On August 7, the government conducted a national referendum on the draft in which a majority of those who voted did so in favor of the draft constitution as well as a second question regarding the selection of the prime minister. The CDC's Referendum Law governed campaigning in the run-up to the referendum. Article 61 of that law provides for a maximum penalty of 10 years' imprisonment for the "dissemination of untrue, provocative, vulgar and aggressive messages through print and electronic media or other channels that could incite unrest." Violations of the Referendum Law are punishable by a maximum 10 years' imprisonment and a maximum fine of 200,000 baht ($5,600).

Officials regularly invoked the law to limit free and open debate in advance of the referendum. According to a government watchdog organization, officials arrested 42 persons and charged them with violating Article 61 of the Referendum Law and arrested approximately 200 additional persons and charged them with related offenses. Human rights groups reported that all those arrested were opponents of the draft charter. As a result numerous national and international observers criticized the referendum as unfair because the electorate was unable to freely receive and impart information and campaign for their choice.

There were no verified reports of irregularities with referendum voting. Voting was held by secret ballot. At the conclusion of voting, precinct officials counted ballots openly. Officials at closed central locations then compiled the precinct vote tallies. At year's end the government had not released official voting results broken down by individual precinct.

Elections and Political Participation

The interim constitution did not provide citizens the ability to choose their government in free and fair periodic elections based on universal and equal suffrage. The 2016 constitution provides citizens the ability to choose their government by voting to elect members to the lower house of parliament. It further provides for the NCPO to appoint members to the upper house for a period of five years, after which members of the upper house will be appointed through a caucus-like system. Both lower and upper house members will select the prime minister, who is not required to be a member of either house. No elections under the new constitution were held by year's end, and the charter awaited promulgation with the signature of King Maha Vajiralongkorn.

Recent Elections: There have been no elections since the 2014 coup. NCPO Announcements No. 85/2557 and No. 86/2557, issued in July 2014, and NCPO Chairman Order No. 1/2557, issued in December 2014, ordered the suspension of all types of elections nationwide, at both the national and local levels.

Political Parties and Political Participation: The interim constitution prohibits anyone who was a member of a political party in the past three years from serving in the NLA. Restrictions on political activity affected political parties' operations.

Participation of Women and Minorities: The precoup constitution encouraged political parties to consider a "close proximity of equal numbers" of both genders. Neither the ruling council's interim constitution nor the 2016 constitution contain such a provision. There were 13 women in the NCPO-appointed 217-member NLA and three female ministers in the 34-person interim cabinet (Ministry of Tourism and Sport, Ministry of Industry, and Ministry of Commerce). The previous elected government had 81 women in the 500-seat lower house.

Few members of ethnic or religious minorities held positions of authority in national politics. The 250-member NLA included four Muslim and two Christian members. The 250-member National Reform Committee included four Muslims, and the 200-member National Reform Steering Committee had four Muslim members. No Muslims or Christians held cabinet posts. All governors in the southernmost provinces were Buddhist, but chief executives in those provincial administrative organizations were Muslim.

Section 4. Corruption and Lack of Transparency in Government

The law provides criminal penalties for conviction of official corruption.
Government implementation of the law increased under the NCPO, although
officials sometimes engaged in corrupt practices with impunity. There were
reports of government corruption during the year.

Corruption: Corruption remained widespread among police. There were
numerous incidents of police charged with abduction, sexual harassment, theft, and
malfeasance, plus reports police tortured, beat, and otherwise abused detainees and
prisoners, generally with impunity. Authorities arrested police officers and
convicted them of corruption, drug trafficking, and smuggling; police reportedly
also committed intellectual property rights violations.

In February the NACC cleared the Royal Thai Army on charges of corruption
related to the construction of Rajbhakti Park.

In February 2015 the attorney general filed criminal charges against former prime
minister Yingluck Shinawatra related to alleged malfeasance in her handling of the
government's rice-pledging program. The trial began in May 2015 and continued
as of October. Several other former Yingluck government officials also faced
criminal charges for their roles in the program.

In addition to criminal charges, numerous former officials also faced civil actions
related to the rice-pledging program. In September the Ministry of Commerce
issued an order to seize assets totaling 20 billion baht ($560 million) from six
former officials found civilly liable for government losses resulting from alleged
fake government-to-government rice deals that formed a part of that program. In
October the Finance Ministry issued a bill to Yingluck Shinawatra for 35.7 billion
baht ($1 billion).

At year's end the government continued to enforce the 2009 arrest warrant against
former prime minister Thaksin Shinawatra. The Supreme Court of Justice for
Persons Holding Political Positions' case against him regarding a 2006 government
bank loan to Burma remained suspended. He continued to reside outside the
country. The NACC and Office of the Auditor General continued to investigate
allegations of corruption committed by members of the Thaksin government from
2001 to 2006, and their findings triggered several cases at the Criminal Division of
the Supreme Court of Justice for Persons Holding Political Positions.

<u>Financial Disclosure</u>: Financial disclosure laws and regulations require elected and appointed public officials to disclose assets and income according to standardized forms. The law penalizes officials who fail to submit declarations, submit inaccurate declarations, or conceal assets. Penalties include a five-year political activity ban, asset seizure, and discharge from position, as well as a maximum imprisonment of six months, a maximum fine of 10,000 baht ($280), or both.

The NACC financial disclosure rules do not apply to NCPO members. Likewise authorities also exempted members of the NCPO-appointed 200-member National Reform Steering Assembly.

<u>Public Access to Information</u>: The law provides for public access to government information, and the government effectively implemented the law. The law provides some exceptions for nondisclosure, including to prevent damage to the monarchy, national security threats, and impediments to effective law enforcement. Regulations require a government agency to respond to a petition within 15 days; however, the regulations do not require it to submit a decision within a certain time. There is no processing fee. If a government agency ignores the petition for disclosure or the requester appeals a request denial, a judge with the Office of the Official Information Commission (OOIC) must decide the case within 60 days. If the OOIC orders the disclosure, the agency must disclose the information within seven days. The law subjects a noncompliant agency head to civil disciplinary actions or criminal penalties. The OOIC received approximately 300 appeals from January to September, which was consistent with 2015 figures. Of the approximately 300 cases received, 230 were completed as of September. The OOIC organized public campaigns and training as well as e-learning programs for officials responsible for reviewing requests.

Section 5. Governmental Attitude Regarding International and Nongovernmental Investigation of Alleged Violations of Human Rights

A wide variety of domestic and international human rights organizations operated in the country. NCPO orders affected NGO operations, including prohibitions on political gatherings and activities as well as media restrictions. NGOs that dealt with sensitive political matters, such as opposition to government-sponsored development projects or border problems, faced periodic harassment.

On September 28, police and Ministry of Labor officials effectively shut down a public event by Amnesty International to roll out a report, *Make Him Speak by*

Tomorrow, documenting allegations of torture and mistreatment by security forces throughout the country. Police and labor officials threatened foreign panelists scheduled to speak at the event with arrest for participating in the event without a work permit. Media and human rights groups condemned the action to shut down the event, arguing that hundreds of foreign persons without work permits regularly participated in nonpolitical events and public seminars without incident.

Human rights workers focusing on violence in the southernmost provinces were particularly vulnerable to harassment and intimidation by government agents and insurgent groups. The government accorded very few NGOs tax-exempt status, which sometimes hampered their ability to secure funding.

The United Nations or Other International Bodies: The government postponed the scheduled visit by the UN special rapporteur on torture and other inhuman treatment. According to UN reports, there were no developments regarding official visits previously requested by the UN working group on disappearances; by the UN special rapporteur on the freedoms of expression, assembly, and association; or by the UN special rapporteur on the situations of human rights defenders, migrants, and internally displaced persons. According to the United Nations, the government has not accepted a visit from any expert within the UN special procedures mechanism since 2013. As of September, 18 visit requests from UN special procedures were pending.

Government Human Rights Bodies: The independent NHRCT exists with the mission to protect human rights and to produce an annual country report. The commission received 617 petitions in the first eight months of the year, compared with 472 in 2015. Of these complaints, 69 related to alleged abuses by police, a sharp increase from the previous year. Statistics regarding completed investigations were unavailable. Civil society leaders rated the NHRCT's performance as moderately better than in previous years, citing constructive NHRCT involvement in working with civil society and the government in conjunction with the UN's universal periodic review process. Human rights groups continued to criticize the commission for not filing lawsuits against human rights violators on its own behalf or on behalf of complainants.

The Office of the Ombudsman is an independent agency empowered to consider and investigate complaints filed by any citizen. Following an investigation the office may refer a case to a court for further review or provide recommendations for further action to the appropriate agency. The office examines all petitions, but it may not compel agencies to comply with its recommendations. Through

September the office received 2,761 new petitions of which 565 related to allegations of police abuses.

Section 6. Discrimination, Societal Abuses, and Trafficking in Persons

Women

<u>Rape and Domestic Violence</u>: Rape is illegal, although the government did not always enforce the law effectively. The law permits authorities to prosecute spousal rape, and prosecutions occurred. Police arrested suspects in 65 percent of sexual assault cases reported from January to mid-September.

The law specifies penalties for conviction of rape or forcible sexual assault ranging from four years' imprisonment to the death penalty as well as fines, depending on such factors as age of the victim, severity of the assault, use of a weapon, participation of multiple assailants, and the physical and mental condition of the victim afterward. The law also provides that any person convicted twice for the same type of criminal rape within three years may receive increased penalties for recidivism. According to court records, authorities filed 3,933 cases involving sexual assault in 2015, compared with 5,310 cases in 2014.

NGOs believed rape to be a serious problem. Academics and women's rights activists maintained that a measure in the law that allows for offenders younger than 18 years to avoid prosecution by choosing to marry their victim constituted a violation of women's rights. They also maintained that victims underreported rapes and domestic assaults, in part due to a lack of understanding by police, prosecutors, and judges of gender and women's rights matters that impeded effective implementation of the law regarding violence against women.

According to NGOs the government underfunded agencies tasked with addressing the problem, and victims often perceived police as incapable of bringing perpetrators to justice. Police sought to change this perception by encouraging women to report sexual crimes. NGOs lobbied for more female investigators in police stations to deal with cases of violence against women, and police made some efforts to increase women's enrollment into the Police Cadet Academy. Female officers constituted approximately 8 percent (or 17,000) of police personnel countrywide, the same as reported in 2015. There were an estimated 300 female police investigators nationwide, with 130 based in Bangkok.

Domestic violence against women was a significant problem. The Ministry of Public Health operated one-stop crisis centers that provide information and services to victims of physical and sexual abuse throughout the country. The law provides authorities, with court approval, the power to prohibit offenders from remaining in their homes or contacting family members during trial. The law also establishes measures designed to facilitate both the reporting of domestic violence complaints and reconciliation between the victim and the perpetrator. Moreover, the law restricts media reporting on domestic violence cases in the judicial system. NGOs voiced concern the law--with a family unity approach--may put undue pressure on a victim to compromise without addressing safety issues and has led to a low conviction rate.

Authorities prosecuted some domestic violence crimes, particularly cases where the perpetrator seriously injured the victim, under provisions for assault or violence against a person, where they could seek harsher penalties. Domestic violence frequently went unreported, however, and police often were reluctant to pursue reports of domestic violence. NGO-supported programs included emergency hotlines, temporary shelters, and counseling services to increase awareness of domestic violence, HIV/AIDS, and other matters involving women. The government operated shelters for domestic violence victims, one in each province. The government's crisis centers, located in all state-run hospitals, cared for abused women and children. Government hospitals referred abused women to private organizations when in-hospital services were not available.

The Ministry of Social Development and Human Security, which collects data on victims who seek legal assistance under the Domestic Violence Prevention Act, reported 363 cases of domestic violence nationwide as of September, compared with 294 cases reported during the first eight months of 2015.

The Ministry of Social Development and Human Security continued to develop a community-based system, operating in all regions of the country, to protect women from domestic violence. The program focused on training representatives from each community on women's rights and abuse prevention to increase community awareness.

Female Genital Mutilation/Cutting (FGM/C): No specific law prohibits this practice. NGOs reported that FGM/C occurred in the Muslim-majority south, although statistics were unavailable. There were no reports of international or governmental efforts to prevent or address the practice.

<u>Sexual Harassment</u>: Sexual harassment is illegal in both the public and private sectors. The law specifies maximum fines of 20,000 baht ($560) for those convicted of sexual harassment. The punishment depends on the degree of harassment. Abuse categorized as an indecent act may result in a maximum 15 years' imprisonment and a maximum fine of 30,000 baht ($840). The penalty depends upon the degree of severity and the age of the victim. The law governing the civil service also prohibits sexual harassment and stipulates five levels of punishment: probation, docked wages, salary reduction, suspension, and termination. NGOs claimed the legal definition of harassment was vague and prosecution of harassment claims difficult, leading to ineffective enforcement of the law. Data on the numbers of abusers prosecuted, convicted, and punished were unavailable.

<u>Reproductive Rights</u>: Couples and individuals have the right to decide the number, spacing, and timing of children; manage their reproductive health; and have access to the information and means to do so, free from discrimination, coercion, or violence. The publicly funded medical system provided access to contraceptive services and information, prenatal care, skilled attendance during childbirth, and essential obstetric and postpartum care.

According to estimates by the United Nations Population Fund (UNFPA), 76 percent of women and girls between 15 and 49 years used a modern contraception method during the year. Officials estimated more than 93 percent of women could access prenatal and postnatal care, and UNFPA reported that skilled health-care personnel attended approximately 100 percent of births. UNFPA estimated the adolescent birth rate was 60 births per 1,000 girls between 15 and 19 years. The Ministry of Education provided sex education in schools, but the rising number of adolescent pregnancies and increases in emergency contraception and unsafe abortions suggested a need to increase access to sexual and reproductive health services, according to UNFPA. Access to health services, including reproductive health, for displaced persons living along the border with Burma was limited.

<u>Discrimination</u>: The interim constitution purported to protect "all human dignity, rights, liberties, and equality of the people." The 2016 constitution provides that "men and women shall enjoy equal rights and liberties. Unjust discrimination against a person on the grounds of differences in origin, race, language, sex, age, disability, physical or health condition, personal status, economic or social standing, religious belief, education or political view, shall not be permitted."

Women generally enjoy the same legal status and rights as men. Nonetheless, women sometimes experienced discrimination. In 2015 the government passed the Gender Equality Act, imposing a maximum jail term of six months or a maximum fine of 20,000 baht ($560), or both, for anyone committing gender discrimination. The law mandates nondiscrimination based on gender and sexual identity in policy, rule, regulation, notification, project, or procedures by government, private organizations, and any individual, but it also stipulates two exceptions criticized by civil society groups: religious principles and national security. Women faced discrimination in employment (see section 7.d.). The law prohibits discriminatory hiring practices common in the workplace, although the law remained untested as of September.

Women were unable to confer citizenship to their noncitizen spouses in the same way as male citizens.

Military academies (except for the nursing academy) refused admittance to female students, although a significant number of instructors were women. According to the Ministry of Defense's Personnel Directorate, 80 women held the rank of general or its equivalent across all military branches and within the Ministry of Defense as of August, a decrease from 96 in 2015. Ministry of Defense policy limits the percentage of female officers to not more than 25 percent in most units, with specialized hospital/medical, budgetary, and finance units permitted 35 percent. During the year the Royal Thai Air Force accepted the first two women into its pilot training program. Women also accounted for approximately 20,700 of the country's 230,000 military personnel.

The Police Cadet Academy for commissioned officers accepted female cadets and reserved 70 of 280 places in the cadet class for women. The first female cadet class graduated from the four-year program in 2013, and four groups of 70 women have graduated from the program and serve throughout the country. According to the Office of the Civil Service Commission, women held 19 percent of executive-level civil service positions (or 211 of 1,097 positions), a slight increase from 2015.

The government designed its Bureau of Women's Affairs and Family Development to promote the legal rights of women, notably under the Bureau of Gender Equality Promotion, but it is not an independent agency. It worked with NGOs, but it did not take a leading role in women's rights.

Children

<u>Birth Registration</u>: Citizenship is conferred at birth if at least one parent is a citizen. Birth within the country does not automatically confer citizenship, but regulations entitle all children born in the country to birth registration, which qualifies them for certain government benefits regardless of citizenship (see section 2.d.). According to NGOs hill tribe members and other stateless persons sometimes did not register births with authorities, especially births occurring in remote areas, because administrative complexities, misinformed or unscrupulous local officials, language barriers, and restricted mobility made it difficult to do so.

<u>Education</u>: Many NGOs reported that children of registered migrant workers, particularly in Samut Sakhon, Kanchanaburi, Ranong, and Chiang Mai Provinces and Mae Sot District of Tak Province, had more limited access to schooling due to frequent relocation to new job sites, distance from school, and a lack of Thai language abilities. Many children attended migrant learning centers at the primary level instead of government schools, which limited migrant students' opportunities beyond primary education because the government did not officially recognize the centers. Migrant children also remained without access to community services provided to children attending public schools, such as day-care centers and government-subsidized free milk and lunch. Migrant workers who could afford it often chose to send their children to private nurseries or day-care centers at their own expense.

<u>Child Abuse</u>: The law provides for the protection of children from abuse, and laws on rape and abandonment carry harsher penalties if the victim is a child. The law imposes a term of seven to 20 years' imprisonment and a maximum fine of 40,000 baht ($1,120) for sexual intercourse with a victim younger than 13 years. If the victim is between 13 and 15 years, the penalty for conviction is four to 20 years' imprisonment and the same range of fines.

Police showed reluctance to investigate abuse cases, and rules of evidence made prosecution of child abuse difficult. The law provides for protection of witnesses, victims, and offenders younger than 18 years in abuse and pedophilia cases. With a judge's consent, children may testify on videotape in private surroundings in the presence of a psychologist, psychiatrist, or social worker. Many judges, however, declined to use videotaped testimony, citing technical problems and the inability to question accusers and defendants directly in court. Some children's advocates claimed sexually abused girls received better physical and psychological care than male victims. Authorities charged persons accused of pedophilia under appropriate age-of-consent laws and, in cases of the commercial sexual exploitation of children, prostitution laws.

<u>Early and Forced Marriage</u>: The minimum legal age for marriage for both sexes is 17 years, while anyone younger than 20 years requires parental consent. A court may grant permission to marry for children between 15 and 16 years. Awareness programs by Islamic committees and government agencies sought to prevent child marriage under Islamic tradition.

NGOs noted that early forced marriage between student teenagers who become pregnant, a practice to "save face" and protect the baby's legal status, appeared to be increasing as the country's teenage pregnancy rate also increased.

<u>Female Genital Mutilation/Cutting (FGM/C)</u>: Information is provided in the Women's subsection above.

<u>Sexual Exploitation of Children</u>: The law provides heavy penalties for persons who procure, lure, compel, or threaten children younger than 18 years for the purpose of prostitution. The law also requires that a customer who purchases sexual intercourse with a child younger than 15 years be subject to two to six years in prison and a maximum fine of 120,000 baht ($3,360). If the child is between 15 and 18 years, the prison term is one to three years and a maximum fine of 60,000 baht ($1,680). Authorities may also punish parents who allow a child to enter into prostitution and revoke their parental rights. The law prohibits the production, distribution, import, or export of child pornography. The penalty for conviction is a maximum imprisonment of three years or a maximum fine of 6,000 baht ($168), or both. The law also imposes heavy penalties on persons convicted of sexually exploiting persons younger than 18 years, including for pimping, trafficking, and other sexual crimes against children.

Child prostitution remained a problem. According to government officials, academics, and NGO representatives, boys and girls, especially among migrant populations and ethnic minorities, were coerced or lured into prostitution. Children from poor families remained particularly vulnerable, and police arrested parents who forced their children into prostitution. Citizens and foreign sex tourists committed pedophilia crimes, including the commercial sexual exploitation of children.

<u>Displaced Children</u>: Authorities generally referred street children to government shelters located in each province, but foreign undocumented migrants avoided the

shelters due to fear of deportation. The government also arrested children, many of whom were trafficking victims, for begging on the streets. The government generally sent citizen street children to school, occupational training centers, or back to their families with social worker supervision. The government repatriated some street children who came from other countries.

National reports on child labor often omitted street children, and national statistics on street children often included only citizens. There was no reliable data on the number of beggars. This population included children who were homeless, kidnapped, or deployed by their parents, and many were trafficking victims.

Institutionalized Children: There were limited reports of abuse in orphanages or other institutions.

International Child Abductions: The country is a party to the 1980 Hague Convention on the Civil Aspects of International Child Abduction. See the Department of State's *Annual Report on International Parental Child Abduction* at travel.state.gov/content/childabduction/en/legal/compliance.html.

Anti-Semitism

The resident Jewish community is very small, and there were no reports of anti-Semitic acts. Nazi symbols and figures were sometimes displayed on merchandise and used in advertising.

Trafficking in Persons

See the Department of State's *Trafficking in Persons Report* at www.state.gov/j/tip/rls/tiprpt/.

Persons with Disabilities

Prior to the 2014 coup, the constitution and law prohibited discrimination against persons with physical, sensory, intellectual, and mental disabilities in education, air travel and other transportation, access to health care, or the provision of other government services. Although coup leaders suspended the constitution, laws pertaining to persons with disabilities remained intact. The 2016 constitution prohibits discrimination based on disability and physical or health conditions.

The government modified many public accommodations and buildings to accommodate persons with disabilities, but government enforcement was not consistent. The law mandates persons with disabilities have access to information, communications, and newly constructed buildings, but authorities did not uniformly enforce these provisions. The law does not require government entities to install accessible street curbs when they repair or construct roads.

The law entitles persons with disabilities who register with the government to free medical examinations, wheelchairs, and crutches. The government provided five-year, interest-free, small-business loans for persons with disabilities.

The government's Community-based Rehabilitation Program and the Community Learning Center for People with Disabilities project operated in all provinces.

The government maintained 46 separate schools for students with disabilities and 77 education centers for persons with disabilities. The law requires all government schools nationwide to accept students with disabilities, and a majority of schools taught students with disabilities during the year. According to the Ministry of Education, an estimated 337,144 students with disabilities attended 48 schools designed specifically for students with disabilities and some of the 213,000 regular schools nationwide. There were also eight government-operated and at least 23 NGO-operated training centers for persons with disabilities, including both full-time and part-time or seasonal centers. The government operated 11 government shelters and nine rehabilitation centers specifically for persons with disabilities, including two day-care centers for autistic children. Private associations also provided occasional training for persons with disabilities.

Some employers subjected persons with disabilities to wage discrimination (see section 7.d.).

National/Racial/Ethnic Minorities

Two groups--former Chinese civil war belligerents and their descendants living in the country for several decades and children of Vietnamese immigrants residing in 13 northeastern provinces--lived under laws and regulations restricting their movement, residence, education, and access to employment. A law confines the Chinese group to residence in the northern provinces of Chiang Mai, Chiang Rai, and Mae Hong Son.

Indigenous People

Noncitizen members of hill tribes faced restrictions on their movement, could not own land, had difficulty accessing bank credit, and faced discrimination in employment. Although labor laws give them the right to equal treatment as employees, employers often violated those rights by paying them less than their citizen coworkers and less than minimum wage. The law also limits noncitizens in their choice of occupations. The law further bars them from government welfare services, such as universal health care.

The law provides citizenship eligibility to certain categories of hill tribes who were not previously eligible. The government supported efforts to register citizens and educate eligible hill tribe members about their rights. Despite such efforts, activists reported widespread corruption and inefficiency, especially among hill tribe village heads and district and subdistrict officials, that contributed to a persistent backlog of citizenship applications and to improperly denied applications. According to the Ministry of the Interior's Department of Provincial Administration, more than 400,000 persons were waiting for authorities to process their citizenship applications.

Hill tribe members faced societal discrimination arising in part from the perception that many of them were involved in drug trafficking, contributed to environmental degradation, and posed a threat to national security.

Acts of Violence, Discrimination, and Other Abuses Based on Sexual Orientation and Gender Identity

No laws criminalize expression of sexual orientation or consensual same-sex sexual conduct between adults.

Lesbian, gay, bisexual, transgender, and intersex (LGBTI) groups could register with the government, although there were some restrictions on terminology used in registering their group names. The LGBTI community reported that police treated LGBTI victims of crime the same as other persons except in the case of sexual crimes, where there was a tendency to downplay sexual abuse or not to take harassment seriously.

The law does not permit transgender persons to change their gender on identification documents, which, coupled with societal discrimination, limited their employment opportunities. The 2015 Gender Equality Act prohibits discrimination "due to the fact that the person is male or female or of a different appearance from his/her own sex by birth."

A local NGO reported that police and military targeted transgender persons for harassment and discrimination in the tourist city of Pattaya, which is known for its transgender performers.

University authorities allowed transgender students to participate in commencement ceremonies and sit for examinations while wearing gender-specific uniforms of their choice on a case-by-case basis. At the same time, university authorities usually required students to obtain official permission before they could wear their chosen uniform. Such permissions remained voluntary at each school.

There was some commercial discrimination based on sexual orientation and gender identity. For example, some life insurance companies refused to issue policies to gay men, although some companies also expressed willingness to sell policies to LGBTI workers with provisions for full transfer of benefits to same-sex partners. NGOs reported more insurance companies began to accept same-sex partner beneficiaries, but this remained at the company's discretion. NGOs alleged some nightclubs, bars, hotels, and factories denied entry or employment to LGBTI individuals, particularly transgender persons.

HIV and AIDS Social Stigma

Persons with HIV/AIDS faced psychological stigma associated with rejection by family, friends, colleagues, teachers, and the community, although intensive educational efforts by the government and NGOs may have reduced this stigma in some communities. There were reports some employers refused to hire persons who tested positive for HIV following employer-mandated blood screening.

Section 7. Worker Rights

a. Freedom of Association and the Right to Collective Bargaining

The interim constitution did not contain provisions providing for the right of freedom of association or the right to bargain collectively. The 2016 constitution requires the state to set up a labor relations system in which all parties may participate. The Labor Relations Act and State Enterprise Labor Relations Act remained in effect. The Labor Relations Act allows private-sector workers to form and join trade unions of their choosing without prior authorization, to bargain collectively, and to conduct legal strikes with a number of restrictions. Under the Labor Relations Act, labor demands can be submitted by workers with the support of at least 15 percent of employees, by unions with the support of at least one fifth of employees, or by the employer. The law prohibits managers or management employees from joining trade unions formed by nonmanagement workers. The law prohibits antiunion discrimination and provides protection to employees and labor unions and their members against criminal or civil charges for carrying out activities (such as negotiation with employers to settle a unions' demand for rights and benefits or organization of a rally or strike activities) for the benefit of its members.

As of December 2015, there were 1,520 trade unions with 634,778 union members (including 180,097 state-owned enterprise (SOE) employees and 454,681 private-sector employees). Union membership represented 3.5 percent of wage and salary workers, up from 3.1 percent in 2007.

The law also allows employees in private enterprises with more than 50 workers to establish "employee committees" to represent workers' collective requests and to negotiate with employers and "welfare committees" to represent workers' collective requests on welfare problems. The law prohibits employers from taking adverse employment actions against workers for their participation in these committees and from obstructing the work of the committees. The Ministry of Labor's Department of Labor Protection and Welfare (DLPW) reported there were 704 employee committees in 2015, down from 945 in 2014.

The State Enterprises Labor Relations Act allows SOE workers to form unions. Each SOE may have a maximum of one union. No law allows civil servants, including teachers at public and private schools, university professors, soldiers, and police, to form or register a union. Civil servants may form and register associations, but these associations do not have the right to bargain collectively. The law forbids strikes and lockouts in the public sector and at SOEs, including those providing services deemed essential to continued public health and safety. The law defines "essential" services more broadly than international norms by including sectors such as telecommunications and public transportation.

Noncitizen migrant workers, whether registered or undocumented, do not have the right to form unions or serve as union officials. Registered migrants may be members of unions organized and led by citizens. Migrant worker participation in unions was limited due to language barriers, weak understanding of rights under the law, frequent changes in employment, restrictive labor union regulations, and segregation of citizen workers from migrant workers by industry and by zones (particularly in border and coastal areas). Nonregistered migrant workers do not have the right to form or join unions.

Union members are not legally protected against antiunion actions by employers until their union is registered. To register a union, at least 10 workers must submit their names to the DLPW. The verification process of vetting the names and employment status with the employer exposes the workers to potential retaliation before registration is complete. Moreover, the law requires that union officials be full-time employees of the company or SOE and prohibits permanent union staff. A union is entitled to no more than two advisors, who must register with the Ministry of Labor.

If a SOE union's membership dips below 25 percent of the eligible workforce, it is subject to administrative dissolution under labor relations regulations. Labor advocates claimed companies exploited this required ratio to avoid unionization by hiring substantial numbers of temporary contract workers.

The law protects employees and union members from criminal or civil charges for participating in negotiations with employers, initiating a strike, organizing a rally, and explaining labor disputes to the public; the law does not protect employees and union members from criminal offenses for endangering the public or for causing loss of life or bodily injury, property damage, and reputational damage. The law does not prohibit lawsuits intended to censor, intimidate, and silence critics through costly legal defense. Private companies charged union leaders with civil and criminal defamation for public statements made during collective bargaining and strike action or for efforts by human rights activists to defend the labor rights of migrant laborers who otherwise faced barriers to unionization and association. Human rights defenders said the use of criminal defamation and other actions to camouflage retaliation had a chilling effect on freedom of expression and association.

Workers have access to the courts to contest wrongful termination. A union leader dismissed for any reason may not continue to represent union members.

The law requires employers to begin negotiating within three days from the time a union submits its demands. The law does not require negotiation in good faith and does not penalize employers who refuse to negotiate after the initial meeting. If the parties cannot reach agreement, the government considers it a labor dispute and begins mandatory conciliation. The law permits workers to strike if a deadlock develops between the employer and employees. Workers must submit a letter of notification at least 24 hours in advance of a strike action. The government has authority to restrict private-sector strikes that would affect national security or cause severe negative repercussions for the population at large, but it did not invoke this provision during the year. There were reports some employers chose to submit counterdemands instead of negotiating based on union demands, which further complicated the negotiation process.

The law prohibits termination of employment of legal strikers but permits employers to hire workers or use subcontract workers to replace strikers. The legal requirement to call a general meeting of trade union members and obtain strike approval by at least 50 percent of union members constrained strike action in the private sector. The law provides for penalties, including a maximum of one year's imprisonment or a fine of 20,000 baht ($560), or both, for strikers in SOEs.

Labor law enforcement was inconsistent, and in some instances ineffective, in protecting workers who participated in union activities. Employers may dismiss workers for any reason except participation in union activities, provided the employer pays severance. Employer discrimination against workers who sought to organize unions included reports of workers dismissed for engaging in union activities, both before and after registration. In some cases labor courts ordered workers reinstated if they proved the grounds for their dismissal were unlawful. The DLPW reported 9,695 unfair dismissal complaints filed with the labor court in 2015, although not all related to union activity. Enforcement of severance payments and reinstatement in cases where authorities found employees were improperly dismissed was inconsistent. Penalties for conviction of labor violations include a maximum of six months' imprisonment, a fine of 10,000 baht ($280), or both, but authorities rarely applied them. Rights advocates reported that labor inspectors at all levels often attempted to mediate cases, even when there was a finding that labor rights violations requiring penalties occurred.

Employees filed grievances in a number of channels, including the tripartite Labor Relations Board, which adjudicates problems of collective labor relations. Its decisions were subject to labor court review. Workers may also seek redress through the NHRCT. The Ministry of Labor may refer private-sector labor disputes that cannot be resolved through negotiation or voluntary arbitration, or that may affect the national economy or public order, to the Labor Relations Board. The State Enterprise Relations Committee handled redress of grievances for SOE workers. During 2015 the DLPW reported 147 informal conflicts between employers and employees involving 106,699 employees, a decrease from 2014

(149 informal conflicts involving 122,474 employees). Of these disputes, employers and employees resolved 121 conflicts without walkouts--the DLPW referred 10 to a labor court, withdrew six cases after negotiation, and continued five under departmental processing. Most cases referred to a labor court fell under the categories of unfair dismissal (46 percent), violations of labor protection laws (27 percent), breaches of working condition agreements (16 percent), and wrongful acts by employers and employees (4 percent). There were a small number of reported violations of social security law and workers' compensation laws.

There were reports employers used various techniques to weaken labor union association and collective bargaining efforts. These included replacing striking workers with subcontractors, which the law permits; threatening union leaders and striking workers; pressuring union leaders and striking workers to resign; prohibiting workers from demonstrating in workplace compounds or in industrial estate zones; and inciting violence in order to get a court warrant to prohibit protests. Under the NCPO there were reports striking workers were threatened with charges of trespassing or violation of public-assembly laws and military officers were present in some negotiation proceedings. Some employers also transferred union leaders and striking workers to different, less desirable positions or inactive management positions (with no management authority) to prevent them from leading union activities. There were reports some employers supported the registration of competing unions to circumvent established unions that refused to accept the terms of agreement proposed by employers.

Legal definitions of who may join a union ("employees working for the same employer" or "employees in the same description of work") and requirements that the union represent at least one-fifth of the workforce hampered collective bargaining efforts. Because the law requires workers be in the same industry to form a union and classifies contract workers as working in the "service industry," as opposed to the "manufacturing industry," they may not join an industrial union despite working in the same factory. This restriction on joining with full-time employees of industries often diminished the ability to bargain collectively as a larger group. The law restricts affiliations between SOE unions and private-sector unions because two separate laws govern them. Labor activists claimed the requirement to get agreement from at least 50 percent of union members created a significant barrier to conducting legal strikes.

b. Prohibition of Forced or Compulsory Labor

The law prohibits all forms of forced or compulsory labor, except in the case of national emergency, war, martial law, or imminent public calamity.

In May the NLA approved the new Human Trafficking Criminal Procedure Act, which expedites the judicial process for trafficking cases, including those of forced labor. The act introduced pretrial deposition and video-conferencing for foreign victims and witnesses and extended the statute of limitations indefinitely. The government's national committee to combat human trafficking, child labor, illegal migration, and illegal fishing began to enforce new laws and regulations in sectors with significant labor concerns. Penalties for conviction under antitrafficking laws amended in 2015 range from four years' to life imprisonment and fines from 80,000 to 400,000 baht ($2,240 to $11,200). The amended antitrafficking law also provides protection to whistle-blowers and gives authoritative power to halt operations temporarily or suspend licenses of businesses and vehicles involved in human trafficking. The lack of clarity in law and practice on what constitutes forced labor or debt bondage undermined the government's efforts to identify labor trafficking victims and prosecute forced labor.

In 2015 the government reported investigating 317 trafficking cases (up from 280 cases in 2014) and prosecuting 242 traffickers (up from 155 in 2014), which resulted in 241 convictions (up from 104 in 2014). The government reported 72 investigations (up from 58 in 2014) involving suspected cases of forced labor and prosecuted 33 cases of forced labor involving 71 suspected traffickers. Of convicted traffickers, 64 percent received prison sentences greater than five years (compared with 29 percent in 2014); 84 percent (68 percent in 2014) received sentences of more than three years. The government established an antitrafficking office within the Criminal Court of Justice and an antitrafficking unit for prosecutors under the Office of the Attorney General.

Reports of abusive work environments, including forced labor, continued in many sectors, including agriculture, fishing, food and seafood processing, and domestic work. Foreign, and often undocumented, migrant labor was common in these sectors; an estimated 90 percent of workers in the seafood processing industry were migrant workers. In 2015 the government investigated ship owners, captains, and brokers for labor trafficking in the fishing industry in 41 cases involving 110 victims, with 31 vessels seized. Two dozen of the cases involved Thai-owned carriers operating in the Indonesian islands of Ambon and Benjina with victims of trafficking from Thailand and neighboring countries. Authorities issued arrest warrants for 98 suspects, 19 of whom authorities arrested as of October. The new antitrafficking criminal court sentenced one broker to 12.5 years in prison; 19 cases remained under prosecution.

In 2015, the most recent year for which information was available, the government identified 720 trafficking victims, compared with 595 victims in 2014. The Ministry of Social Development and Human Security reported assisting 471 victims at government shelters (compared with 303 in 2014), including 320 victims of forced labor.

Civil society observers criticized government handling of vulnerable migrant workers and undocumented migrants who may have been victims of human trafficking. Lack of legal status, ability to organize, Thai language literacy, and an understanding of local law, along with language barriers and ineffective complaint mechanisms for non-Thai speakers, increased vulnerability to exploitation for the large numbers of migrants from Burma, Cambodia, and Laos.

Migrant workers often assumed debts to informal labor brokers or local moneylenders, some of whom charged interest rates as high as 20 percent. These practices led migrant workers, in some cases, into conditions of debt bondage. Migrant labor advocates reported that employers, subcontractors, and brokers (both formal and informal) charged excessive fees to workers to acquire documentation, such as transportation or identity documents from origin countries, exacerbating vulnerability to debt bondage. There were reports some employers confiscated migrant registration cards, work permits, and travel documents of migrant workers, thus restricting internal movement and contributing to their vulnerability to forced labor with little recourse under the law. Work permits that tied workers to a single employer and required burdensome procedures to change an employer made it difficult for migrant workers to leave unscrupulous employers. The law limited noncitizens in their choice of occupation. To avoid deportation, illegal migrants often paid additional fees or bribes to police and immigration officers.

Some workers on fishing vessels were reportedly unable to return to shore, and their employers forced them to continue working in harsh conditions with low pay and very limited protection and benefits. The Labor Protection Act ministerial regulations require employees in fishing vessels to receive regular wages and rest periods and to report to labor inspectors at least once per year. The 2015 Royal Ordinance on Fisheries imposes sanctions, including fines or revocation of business licenses, for vessels that violate labor protections laws or employ undocumented migrant workers. Migrant labor rights organizations reported a shortage of interpreters, ineffectual inspection techniques, and a lack of clear understanding among officials of new laws and procedures regulating fishing vessels crippled the effectiveness of inspection efforts on sea-going vessels.

Also see the Department of State's *Trafficking in Persons Report* at www.state.gov/j/tip/rls/tiprpt/.

c. Prohibition of Child Labor and Minimum Age for Employment

The law regulates the employment of children younger than 18 years and prohibits employment of children younger than 15 years. Employers may not require children younger than 18 years to work overtime or on a holiday and may not require work between 10 p.m. and 6 a.m. without prior Ministry of Labor approval. Children younger than 18 years must not be employed in hazardous work, which includes: any activity involving metalwork, hazardous chemicals, poisonous materials, radiation, and harmful temperatures or noise levels; exposure to toxic microorganisms; operation of heavy equipment; work underground or underwater; and work in prohibited workplaces, such as slaughterhouses, gambling establishments, places where alcohol is sold, or massage parlors. The law provides limited coverage to child workers in some informal sectors, such as agricultural farming, and allows for issuance of ministerial regulations to address sectors not covered.

In 2014 the Ministry of Labor increased the minimum age for agricultural work from 13 to 15 years and for work on sea-fishing vessels from 16 to 18 years. In January the DLPW prohibited children younger than 18 years from employment in seafood processing factories and establishments. The laws do not specify the maximum number of hours per day children between 15 and 17 years may legally perform agricultural or domestic work.

The government approved the second phase of its *National Policy and Plan to Eliminate the Worst Forms of Child Labor*, which aims to eradicate child labor in the country by 2020 and includes a three-year action plan to achieve this goal. In an effort to strengthen criminal legislation against the commercial and sexual exploitation of children, the government adopted an amendment to criminalize the production, distribution, and possession of child pornography.

The maximum penalties for conviction of violating child labor laws or regulations is one year in prison or a fine of 200,000 baht ($5,600), or both. The Social Security Office under the Ministry of Labor reported 49,263 children between 15 and 17 years formally working and registered in the social security system in 2014, the latest year for which this data was available. The total estimate of child laborers, legal and illegal, continued to be much larger when it included child laborers in the informal sector, including illegal migrants.

The DLPW and the National Statistical Office issued the country's first national report on working children in August. The survey found that common hazardous conditions for children included lifting heavy objects, exposure to hazardous temperatures or loud noises, and exposure to dangerous chemical and radioactive substances, such as pesticide or fireworks. Most working children were employed in agriculture, forestry, fisheries, wholesale retail trade, hotels, restaurants, and manufacturing. The government began collaborating with the International Labor Organization (ILO) to ensure future surveys meet globally recognized standards.

The DLPW is the primary agency charged with enforcing child labor laws and policies. In 2015 the DLPW increased efforts to inspect workplaces in the informal sector and found child labor violations in a variety of activities, including food and beverage services, construction, manufacturing, and seafood processing. As a result of these inspections, authorities removed 22 children from unlawful employment. Violations included employing underage child labor, unlawful working hours, and failure to notify the DLPW of employment of child workers between 15 and 17 years. The maximum penalties for conviction of employment of children in hazardous conditions or in prohibited workplaces under the Labor Protection Act is one year in prison or a 200,000 baht ($5,600) fine, or both. While authorities generally subjected child labor law violators to fines, the penalties for conviction were usually less than the maximum penalty prescribed by law. The Ministry of Labor took steps to address the problem by promulgating internal regulations requiring the application of maximum penalties for violations of child labor laws. Observers noted several limiting factors in effective enforcement of child labor laws, including: insufficient labor inspectors, lack of nationwide data or systems to evaluate child labor conditions, and ineffective inspection procedures for informal sector or hard-to-reach workplaces (such as private residences, small family-based business units, farms, and fishing boats). Moreover, a lack of public understanding of child labor laws and standards for hazardous work for children, including dangers from pesticides, heat, and machinery, played a vital role in allowing children to work, particularly in agricultural work or in family-based businesses.

Employers paid some children to fight in Thai boxing matches with no protective equipment. Employers used child labor to produce some garments, plant and harvest sugarcane, and process shrimp, fish, and sugarcane. In urban areas most working children labored in the service sector, including in gasoline stations, small-scale industries, and restaurants. Some children were also sexually exploited as part of the commercial sex and pornography trade. Employers subjected migrant children to forced labor in fishing, production of garments, food and seafood processing, domestic service, and panhandling. Many of these children, predominantly migrants from Burma, Cambodia, and Laos, were in the country illegally, which increased their vulnerability to exploitation.

There were reports children were allegedly bought, rented, or forcibly "borrowed" from their parent(s) or guardian(s) to beg alongside women in the street. Reports also indicated some parents, particularly migrant parents, deployed children to beg during school break, evenings after school, or on weekends to contribute to household income. The revised Begging Control Act, which came into effect in July, enhanced services for beggars and outlawed using, hiring, promoting, or urging others to beg.

Child labor was less evident but still present in larger, export-oriented factories and registered processing facilities, including multiple levels of the food and seafood processing sectors. There were reports some working children were undocumented and did not have employment contracts or that they obtained passports or migrant registration cards from authorities with a falsified age. Despite legal prohibitions children younger than 18 years were exposed to hazardous conditions, such as work with fire, heat, or strong sunlight; damp, malodorous, and dirty workplaces; long working hours (more than eight hours per day); dusty workplaces; hazardous tools; environments with extreme temperatures; and overnight shifts.

There continued to be reports insurgent groups recruited children to commit acts of arson or serve as scouts and informants or to involve them in village defense militias.

Migrant children had access to government schools. The Ministry of Education reported enrollment of noncitizens in public schools increased by 38 percent, from 99,933 students in 2012 to 138,724 students in 2015. Migrant children faced widely varied impediments to enrollment due to language barriers, frequent mobility of migrant parents pursuing seasonal work, lack of awareness of their right to public education or low cultural acceptance, and lack of reciprocity with home-country education systems. In the face of these constraints, parents often enrolled their children in NGO-operated migrant learning centers.

Also see the Department of Labor's *Findings on the Worst Forms of Child Labor* at www.dol.gov/ilab/reports/child-labor/findings/.

d. Discrimination with Respect to Employment and Occupation

In previous years, labor laws did not prohibit discrimination in the workplace regarding race, sex, gender, disability, language, political opinion, religion, age, social origin, national origin or citizenship, sexual orientation or gender identity, HIV-positive status or other communicable diseases, or social status. In September the 2014 Gender Equality Act came into effect, imposing a maximum jail term of six months, a maximum fine of 20,000 baht ($560), or both, for anyone committing gender or gender identity discrimination, including in employment decisions. Another law requires workplaces with more than 100 employees hire at least one worker with disabilities for every 100 workers. The government did not effectively enforce these laws in all cases.

Discrimination with respect to employment occurred against LGBTI persons, migrant workers, and women (see section 7.e.). Government regulations require employers to pay equal wages and benefits for equal work, regardless of gender. Nonetheless, women received lower pay for equal work in many sectors of the economy. Employers did not allow women to work in all industries available to men. Discrimination against persons with disabilities occurred in employment, access, and training. As of 2014 the government reported that 9,454 of 12,479 enterprises (approximately 76 per cent) complied with the obligations contained in the Persons with Disabilities Empowerment Act.

Although it remained unclear what practical effect the 2014 Gender Equality Act might have, in recent years persons of diverse sexual orientations and gender identities in the country faced frequent discrimination in the workplace, partly due to common prejudices and a lack of protective laws and policies on discrimination. A 2014 ILO report found discrimination at all stages of the employment process, including education and training, access to jobs, advancement opportunities, social security, and partner benefits. Transgender workers reportedly faced even greater constraints, and their participation in the workforce was often limited to a few professions, such as beauticians and entertainers.

e. Acceptable Conditions of Work

The national daily minimum wage remained at 300 baht ($8.40). The government last calculated the official poverty line in 2014 at 2,647 baht ($74) per month. In

May the government also announced standard wages for skilled laborers ranging from 340 to 550 baht ($10 to $15) per day. The law on minimum wage does not apply to laborers in seasonal agriculture or domestic work.

The maximum workweek by law is 48 hours, or eight hours per day over six days, with an overtime limit of 36 hours per week. Employees engaged in "dangerous" work, such as chemical, mining, or other industries involving heavy machinery, may work a maximum of 42 hours per week and may not work overtime. Petrochemical industry employees may not work more than 12 hours per day and may work continuously for a maximum period of 28 days. By law employers may not change employment conditions without the employee's consent, unless the changes benefit the employee.

The law requires safe and healthy workplaces, including for home-based businesses, and prohibits pregnant women and children younger than 18 from working in hazardous conditions (as detailed in ministerial regulations). The law allows pregnant women to present a physician's certificate to request a change of duties both prior to and after delivery. The law also requires the employer to inform employees about hazardous working conditions prior to employment. Workers do not have the right to remove themselves from situations that endangered health or safety without jeopardy to their employment.

Legal protections do not apply equally to all sectors. For example, ministerial regulations provide household domestic workers some protections regarding holidays, sick leave, minimum age, and payment of wages, but they do not address minimum wage, regular working hours, or maternity leave. The minimum wage and social security system does not apply to workers in the informal sector and seasonal types of work, such as agriculture. Although the Home Based Worker Protection Act came into force in 2011, the DLPW has not yet issued regulations on wages, working conditions, and prohibited hazardous work for home-based workers.

The DLPW is responsible for verifying that employers adhere to minimum wage requirements in the formal sector as well as inspecting working hours, rest time, holiday and sick leave, and overtime payment. The DLPW also enforces laws related to labor relations and occupational safety and health. The law subjects employers to maximum fines of 100,000 baht ($2,800) and a maximum imprisonment of six months for minimum wage noncompliance, but enforcement was inconsistent. The maximum sentence for conviction of violations of occupational safety and health regulations is one year's imprisonment and fines of

400,000 baht ($11,200). In 2015 there were approximately 350,961 workplaces employing 8.4 million workers. This estimate did not include informal workplaces, such as family farms and home-based businesses. The DLPW had only 592 labor inspectors nationwide, insufficient to enforce labor laws.

DLPW labor inspectors inspected 44,859 workplaces employing 1.6 million workers during 2015 and found that 663 workplaces failed to comply with labor protection laws. In response, 624 orders were issued, nine employers were subjected to fines, and 30 employers were subjected to criminal charges. Labor inspections took place in various industries but mostly focused on wholesale retail trade (37 percent) and manufacturing (22 percent) with fewer inspections conducted in informal workplaces, such as construction (6 percent) and agriculture (2 percent). Most violations involved failure to pay minimum wage and overtime and holiday pay, failure to provide traditional or annual holidays, failure to provide and announce work rules, and failure to keep records of employee wage payment and hours worked. In 2015 the DLPW received 594 demands from 502,976 employees and 114 labor dispute cases involving 104,654 employees. Limited numbers of inspectors, the practice of interviewing employees at workplace locations, reliance on document-based inspection, and lack of interpreters to accompany inspection teams resulted in ineffective inspections.

On occupational health and safety, in 2015 the DLPW inspected 16,538 workplaces employing 946,621 workers and found that 1,312 workplaces (8 percent) failed to comply with health and safety regulations. Most of these involved failure to establish safety committees; problems with machines, cranes, and boilers; health checkups; and inappropriate levels of heat, light, and noise in construction areas. According to the DLPW, the highest numbers of violations regarding workers' safety occurred in the manufacturing, wholesale and retail trade, construction, and hotel and restaurant industries. After the department issued orders to companies to make amends, companies resolved the majority of violations, although labor inspectors filed at least 189 legal actions after employers failed to make amends or pay the required fine.

Redress for workers injured in industrial accidents generally was untimely and insufficient. Court decisions were rare, and seldom went against management or owners, but isolated cases demonstrated the courts have legal authority to compensate injured workers. NGOs reported several cases of the government denying accident compensation to registered migrants because they had not passed nationality verification. In September 2015 the Supreme Administrative Court ruled to rescind a regulation issued by the Social Security Office that it deemed set out unlawful practices and discriminatory treatment against migrant workers and their access to the Workmen's Compensation Fund. The court ruled that registered migrants allowed to work temporarily in the country should be entitled to accident compensation.

Some workers received less than the minimum wage, particularly in rural provinces and in enterprises employing less than 50 workers. Labor unions estimated 30 percent of workers received less than the minimum wage. Labor protections apply to undocumented workers, but many employers did not provide the minimum wage to unskilled and semi-skilled undocumented migrant workers. A large income gap remained between formal and informal employment, with workers in the nonagricultural sector earning an average of three times more than those in the agricultural sector. A reported 55 percent of the labor force worked in the informal economy, including in agriculture, forestry, and fishing, with limited protection under labor laws and the social security system.

While there was no reliable count of illegal migrant workers in the country, government and NGO sources estimated the number of both registered and illegal migrant workers to be 2.5 to 3.9 million.

Despite efforts at regularization and renewal of work permits, migrant workers, in particular undocumented migrants, did not enjoy many labor protections accorded to citizen workers and remained vulnerable and without recourse under the law. NGOs reported poor working conditions for both documented and undocumented migrant workers. A substantial number of migrants worked in factories near border-crossing points, where there were frequent reports of labor law violations. In February the government introduced a policy allowing registered migrant workers to renew their work permits every two years for a maximum of eight years without the need to return to their country of origin. This policy reduced the cost and burden for migrant workers and increased incentives for them to register. The Ministry of Labor hired nine full-time, bilingual telephone hotline operators since 2014. The number of migrant worker calls to these hotlines increased significantly. In 2015 Ministry of Labor hotlines received 105,505 calls, of which 79,494 were from Thai speakers and 26,011 were by non-Thai speakers. Most non-Thai callers sought information on the migrant worker registration process, changing employers or workplaces, and work permit renewals. A limited number of calls were complaints regarding labor law violations.

Companies employing migrant workers reportedly made unlawful deductions from migrant worker wages to repay the costs of cross-border travel, registration, permits, and other expenses. Workers also reported several other violations by contractors, including failure to pay holiday overtime; provide equipment, uniforms, or adequate drinking water; or pay daily minimum wages for less than eight hours of work. Workers further reported deductions from wages for sick leave absences and bribes to officials to ignore undocumented workers.

The government requires employers in the fishing industry to keep official records of their workers and worker payroll records as well as to use standardized employment contracts that clearly outline the wage, working hours, benefits, and provisions for welfare while working on board a vessel. The 2014 ministerial regulations for sea-fishing vessels requires the income of fishery workers (base salary plus share from profit) to be equal to the national minimum wage. The law also requires rest periods and annual and holiday leave. It further requires employers to take workers to report to the Ministry of Labor at least once per year. Furthermore, the regulation requires employers to pay at least 50 percent of the daily wage during periods when workers are outside the country without work and unable to return to the country. The new law also mandates that employers cover transportation costs to return workers to a recruitment area if their boat was not operational, if workers are unable to work, if the employer alters or terminates the employment contract before the end of the contract, or when the employment contract ends. Nonetheless, workers in the fishing industry lacked access to social security and accident compensation. To strengthen enforcement in the fishing sector, the government established 28 port-in-port-out (PIPO) centers to check documents and monitor and inspect vessels and workers. As of September multidisciplinary teams led by the Royal Thai Navy inspected 13,504 workers on 999 fishing vessels and found wrongdoing on 25 vessels. Of these, authorities subjected 23 employers to administrative orders and penalties and filed lawsuits against two.

The government previously required local agencies that recruit migrant workers to come into the country to register with the Ministry of Labor's Department of Employment (DOE). As of September, 274 in-bound recruitment agencies had registered with the DOE. The Royal Ordinance on Importation of Foreign Workers to Work in Thailand took effect in August. The law requires employment agents to inform migrant workers of wage and other benefit information. They must also publish service fees at a rate no higher than 25 percent of the first month's wages. Employers must pay service fees, costs of transportation to and from the home country, and other associated fees. Employment agents must deposit a five million baht ($140,000) "guarantee" fee, which the DOE is to use as a compensation fund for assisting workers, as needed.

Labor brokerage firms used a "contract labor system" under which workers sign an annual contract. By law businesses must provide contract laborers "fair benefits and welfare without discrimination." Regardless of whether the contract labor employee was outsourced and collected wages from a separate company, by law the contracting business is the overall employer, and the law requires equal pay and benefits for subcontract and regular employees. Although contract laborers performed the same work as direct-hire workers, employers often paid them less and provided fewer or no benefits.

NGOs noted local moneylenders, mostly informal, offered loans at exorbitant interest rates so citizen workers looking for work abroad could pay recruitment fees, some as high as 500,000 baht ($14,000). DOE regulations limit the maximum charges for recruitment fees, but effective enforcement of the rules remained difficult and inadequate due to workers' unwillingness to provide information and the lack of legal documentary evidence (loan agreement or written service or lending contract) regarding underground recruitment fees. The DOE regulates in-bound and out-bound recruitment agencies. In 2015 the DOE found bad practices in 10 registered recruitment agencies, subsequently suspending three agencies and filing criminal charges against seven. The DOE also worked with police to investigate 287 complaints from citizen workers employed outside the country. Exploitative employment service agencies persisted in charging citizens working overseas large, illegal recruitment fees that frequently equaled their first- and second-year earnings. Police charged 68 illegal brokers for deceiving people in exchange of money under the Employment and Job-Seeker Protection Act, which allows for a maximum penalty of 10 years in prison and/or a maximum fine of 200,000 baht ($5,600).

In 2014, the latest year for which data was available, there were 100,234 reported incidents of diseases and injuries from workplace accidents, including 68,903 minor injuries (resulting in no more than three workdays missed) and 31,331 injuries resulting in more than three workdays missed (including permanent disabilities and deaths). Observers said workplace accidents in the informal and agricultural sectors and among migrant workers were underreported. Employers rarely diagnosed or compensated occupational diseases, and few doctors or clinics specialized in them. Migrant workers and their dependents in both the formal and informal sectors were eligible to buy health insurance. Some migrant workers, however, did not purchase health insurance because they did not understand their rights due to language barriers, an insufficient number of health-care personnel, and other factors. Medium and large factories often applied government health and safety standards, but overall enforcement of safety standards was lax. In the informal sector, health and safety protections were substandard.